FOREWORD BY BISHOP EASTON GRANT

BY HIS DESIGN

RUFUS MAHON

12 MEN, 1 GOD & A LEGACY OF PURPOSE

THIS IS A WRITTEN WORK BY
RUFUS G. MAHON & THE BY HIS DESIGN MEN'S COLLECTIVE
PUBLISHED BY DAUGHTERS OF DEBORAH PUBLISHING

This book is based on the divinely inspired thoughts and life experiences
of **Rufus G. Mahon** and **The By His Design Men's Collective**.
All content therein is written as recalled and recounted by them.
All identities are used by permission or purposely omitted to protect the
privacy of those living or dead.

BY HIS DESIGN

www.AllisonMahonMinistries.com

Library of Congress Cataloging-In-Publication Number
PENDING

ISBN 979-8-9920189-5-0

First Edition Printing

Printed in the United States of America

October 2025

DEDICATION

THIS COLLECTION OF WRITINGS IS DEDICATED TO MEN EVERYWHERE WHO HAVE A STORY THAT THEY HAVE NOT TOLD YET. MEN THAT ARE STRIVING, BUT YET HAVE GONE UNNOTICED, MEN THAT HAVE NOT BEEN CELEBRATED AND FEEL OVERLOOKED. THIS BOOK I DEDICATE TO THE EVERYDAY MAN THAT IS HOLDING IT TOGETHER DAILY, THIS BOOK IS FOR YOU.

By HIS Design

BEFORE I FORMED YOU IN THE WOMB I KNEW YOU

JEREMIAH 1:5

TABLE OF CONTENTS

5

Acknowledgements

Writing this book has truly been a journey filled with balance, sacrifice, and perseverance. Finishing it required me to handle many responsibilities at once, and it wouldn't have been possible without the unwavering support, encouragement, and guidance of many remarkable individuals. Many of you may never realize how much your presence, prayers, and words helped steady and strengthen me along the way.

It would be a disservice for me to try to name everyone, as I risk unintentionally missing someone. Instead, I want to thank God for each person He strategically placed in my life to help, pour into, and push me forward, often in unconventional ways.

To my wife, your patience, understanding, and persistent encouragement not to give up served as the foundation for this work. You are my greatest supporter and the quiet force that kept me moving when I wanted to pause.

To my four sons, watching you grow, face challenges, and mature into young men has inspired me more than you realize. This book is part of the legacy I wish to leave for you, something you can draw from as you continue your journeys.

To my spiritual sons, whose hunger for wisdom often sparks my own reflections, your questions and growth have profoundly shaped this writing as well.

To my friends and mentors, thank you for your honesty and insight. Even in casual conversations, your words pushed me to think more deeply, live better, and aim higher. Your wisdom has been priceless throughout this journey.

I especially appreciate the men who shared their stories, experiences, and perspectives so openly. Your honesty added authenticity and depth to these pages that couldn't have been achieved otherwise.

To every reader, thank you for your interest and willingness to embark on this journey through these words. My hope is that this book inspires, informs, and empowers you to walk confidently in your own purpose.

Finally, to everyone who believed in this project from the very beginning—The LEGNA Agency, In His Image, Daughters of Deborah, and Bishop Easton Grant—your faith in me made all the difference. From my heart, thank you.

Rufus

FOREWORD

It is with great joy and reverence that I commend to you this powerful work, *By His Design: 12 Men. One God. A Legacy of Purpose.* At seventy-six years of age, having served as a pastor for fifty-six of those years, I can testify with conviction that the Word of God remains eternal and unshaken. I have lived long enough to see men wrestle with issues of identity, leadership, integrity, and purpose. Yet, I have also seen, time and again, the transforming power of God's blueprint when a man fully surrenders to it.

This book is more than a collection of stories—it is a prophetic witness. Within these pages, you will encounter men who allowed God to meet them in their brokenness, shape them through trials, and release them into lives of destiny. Each testimony reveals the process of becoming—not merely in title, but in true transformation. Together, they affirm that manhood, when aligned with God's original design, is a calling of eternal consequence.

I know this path well. Early in my own journey, I believed that success in ministry was measured by crowds, buildings, or titles. But the Lord, in His mercy, stripped away my pride and rebuilt me in His truth. He taught me to unlearn the lies of culture that equate manhood with power, control, or recognition. Instead, I came to embrace the reality that true manhood is rooted in servanthood, stewardship, and sonship in Christ.

Over the years, I have watched God raise up men who once wandered without direction, only to become builders of homes, leaders of churches, and pillars within their communities. I have seen men discover that legacy is not defined by what you leave in your hands but by what you impart into the hearts of others. That is the power of living according to His design.

To the next generation, I offer this charge: hold fast to the truth of God's Word. Refuse to let the shifting sands of culture define who you are. Walk with integrity. Cherish your families. Be accountable to one another. And remember always that you are God's masterpiece, created anew in Christ Jesus for the good works He prepared long ago (*Ephesians 2:10*).

May this book inspire you, convict you, and challenge you to rise to your God-given purpose. And may it remind you that becoming a man by His design is not about perfection, but about surrender. In that surrender, you will find strength, direction, and a legacy that will outlive you.

With gratitude and expectation,

Bishop Easton G. Grant

76 Years Young · 56 Years a Shepherd

LEGACY OVER LABELS

BISHOP
RUFUS MAHON

Legacy or labels? This is a question that many men quietly face and have to decide on daily. To understand this, let's define each one so we can move forward from there.

According to the dictionary, **legacy** can be defined as "the long-lasting impact of a particular event(s), actions, etc., that took place in the past, or of a person's life." Legacy can also be defined as "something transmitted by or received from an ancestor or predecessor or from the past."

From this definition, we see that legacy is what we pass on to someone. Legacy isn't just about money; it includes behaviors, actions, and memories that leave a lasting impact on others or on something from us. Now, let's examine the definition of a label.

According to the dictionary, label can be defined as "a small piece of paper, fabric, plastic or similar material attached to an object and giving information about it." Label can also be defined as "a classifying phrase or name applied to a person or thing, especially one that is inaccurate or restrictive." From these definitions, we see that labels are given by others and applied to a person, place, or object. These judgments can be inaccurate and may also impose limited boundaries on how the object or person can operate.

Now that we have a clear definition of legacy and labels, let's discuss each one and how it relates to us. When we review the above definitions, we see that legacy influences all aspects of our lives. Legacy is in our thoughts, our mannerisms, the way we choose our friends, and even the places where we decide to work.

Legacy is present in our daily moments as we go through our days. You may ask yourself, why is that? It is this way because legacy has been imparted into you before you were born.

We observe this in the family line of the Patriarch Abraham. Abraham had a few tendencies in his life that were common. One in particular stood out when he was under pressure. That was especially noticeable because his inability to not tell the truth happens to all of us. When it becomes a subconscious habit, we can attribute it to legacy behavior. We don't know exactly where Abraham inherited this pattern, but we can assume it was from his father, Terah, who worshipped idols.

We understand that Satan, known as the Father of lies, reveals to us that he was the one who began not telling the truth in the Garden of Eden, and all lies can be traced back to him. Satan is the one whose legacy we can follow. When we open ourselves to influences, we never know what is being imparted in that moment. Remember, one of the definitions of legacy we mentioned is "something transmitted by or received from an ancestor or predecessor or from the past." Satan is the predecessor, the ancestor, or the forefather of lies. When Abraham lied, it was because of the predecessor who stepped into the lifestyle of Terah, who worshipped idols and took on the nature of the Father of lies. From there, we see the legacy of lies being passed down. Abraham lied about Sarah being his wife, Isaac lied about Rebekah being his wife, and Jacob was coached into lying by his mother, Rebekah.

She is the same person who was lied about and is now coaching others on how to lie. Jacob, who was later named Israel, had twelve sons and one daughter. Eleven of those sons devised a lie to hide what they did to their youngest brother Joseph. Dinah, Jacob's daughter, was "treated unfairly," and her brothers Simeon and Levi lied to get even with the young man who "treated her unfairly." We can see how this legacy was passed down until someone appeared to interrupt this ungodly pattern and become the progenitor of a godly, righteous legacy. When we reflect on our lives, what kind of legacy are we leaving for others? Remember, legacy isn't about money, houses, or cars; it's about behaviors, mindsets, and choices we make daily that shape our lives from day to day, month to month, year to year, and decade to decade.

Allow me to have a transparent moment.

Most of my life, I have lived in shame. Let me define shame so you can understand where I am coming from. Shame can be described as an emotion that involves a negative self-

14

assessment, where I believe something is fundamentally wrong with me.

This negative self-evaluation developed early because I stuttered. Many people don't understand the psychological trauma that those who stutter experience. The questions that constantly haunt me include "why Rufus, you just can't talk like everybody else," "Rufus, be careful, you don't want to embarrass yourself," and even a feeling that something is indescribably wrong with me because I stutter.

At one point in my life, I believed that God was angry with me, which is why I stuttered. As you can see from these examples, there is an ongoing internal dialogue behind the eyes of someone who stutters. Then there's the psychological cruelty of others who mock you because you stutter, and this adds to the shame.

Shame is feeling embarrassed or guilty because of your actions, traits, or associations. Now, I feel shame about how I look and sound when I stutter, which only lowers my self-esteem and feeds the shame inside me. This cycle of mental torment I have endured from a young age. It didn't help that my biological father made fun of me face-to-face for stuttering.

Even now, I sometimes struggle with the negative words spoken to me in childhood that still echo in my mind today. I have to fight those voices and thoughts whenever they appear, or they will cause chaos in my life.

The shame or ashamed cycle that I labeled myself with was a daily occurrence that continued well into my adult years. This self-imposed label fueled many decisions until I finally broke the cycle.

Let me explain: the many years I spent "self-proving" that I wasn't what my verbal abusers said. Yes, verbal abuse can be disguised as "just making fun of," but to the person on the receiving end of this verbal assault, the outcome is shame or feeling ashamed. Believe it or not, those spoken words help reinforce the label placed upon me. I lacked the skills to fight back against what was spoken externally and struggled internally.

This led me to try to prove the opposite to others. This self-proving behavior looked like being the proverbial "player," showing myself that because I could attract many girls or women, I could also identify as "one of the guys." I didn't realize that I was already caught in a cycle, with shame as the vehicle I was riding in, and every time I opened the door, I felt ashamed and climbed back into that shame. One thing I didn't realize was that because I was stuck in this cycle, I was also teaching others to do the same, and that's what legacy is about. It's not so much what I leave you, but what I deposit in you, and I realized that wasn't the legacy I wanted to leave in those around me. This became clearer once I understood what I passed on to my children.

We often want to start college funds when a child is born or put their names on insurance papers in case something tragic happens, or do anything else that can improve their material wellbeing. We really don't focus enough on what we emphasize inside our children, like character, integrity, morals, or self-esteem. These qualities are developed and built within the structure of the family. When the family becomes disorganized due to violence, divorce, or even drug abuse, this gets passed down to the children. Some may call it generational curses, but I want to say it's a generational legacy in action.

When I began to realize this, I knew I didn't want to leave this earth with all the broken pieces still inside me. I understood I desired change and needed to take the first step toward it.

This transformative mindset came after I accepted Christ into my life. The help I needed came from that initial step. Even after accepting Christ, it couldn't stop there. Many people believe that accepting Christ solves all their problems, but honestly, it doesn't.

There's still plenty of work because now I must align my life with the Word of God, and that's the difficult part. This alignment helps break the cycle of generational legacies of struggle and begins a new legacy of wholeness in God.

Let me clarify: it's not enough to simply attend church on Sundays and stop there. Honestly, that's only the start of the legacy process. As I mentioned earlier, legacy isn't just about leaving material things to improve someone's earthly wellbeing; it's about what you instill in someone to uplift their mental, emotional, and spiritual health.

One day, it hit me—do I want my children to grow up like me, or do I want them to grow up better than I did? When that realization came, I knew the shameful legacy I've been living in had to be broken. I no longer want to see myself through someone else's eyes. I decided I no longer want to live for anyone's approval except Christ's. To do this, I must admit it's not easy, but it's possible by making a daily choice to live this way.

There were obstacles and hurdles I faced regularly. These sometimes challenged me to go back to old ways of doing things. When I heard people say, "I'm in the fight of my life," I understood what that meant. Breaking free from that legacy I was taught is not easy when it's all I've known for so long. Now, to engage in this new process, I had to learn a new way of life—one that required me to leave behind old lifestyles and behaviors I was so used to, and to adopt a new way of living and acting that I wasn't familiar with. For me, this was extremely uncomfortable.

In the book I wrote called *A Wolf in Sheep's Clothing*, I provided a detailed look at the lifestyle I used to live. On one occasion, when I first committed to a new way of living, the "boys" I used to hang out with tried to set me up several times.

This involved sending my old appetites my way to tempt me to revert back to the old ways. Let me say this: change doesn't happen overnight, and it's hard-fought. Just because I decided to change didn't mean everyone around me would accept my changes or encourage me to keep going. Oh no! Instead, I faced resistance from those I once called my friends.

I had built a culture, a legacy that I believed I wanted to leave behind. One that was centered around being "The Man," defined by my sexual conquests and desires. When I decided to stop and break ranks, it meant challenging that division and threatening the so-called legacy. There were times when what I liked was intentionally sent my way, and when that didn't work, the name-calling that followed was meant to make me fall back into line. Sometimes, others will try to shame you into a legacy that isn't truly yours or that you're trying to break free from.

Many may call it peer pressure or by another name, but it's really the tool of shame being used to steer a person away from what is right for them. Remember, shame is defined as a negative self-evaluation, feeling that something is fundamentally wrong with you. When I realized that shame was being used to keep me ashamed, which made me feel guilty for wanting to be different, I felt deep inside that I was longing for something different. That was when I knew I was on the right track. Let me go a little further into this:

Even after entering the "church," there was still a lot of shaming happening inside. I looked at others and felt like "because I am not like them, something is wrong with me." For many years, I struggled to fit in but was never successful. This left me feeling ashamed, which caused me to struggle to be something I was never meant to be. When a legacy is placed inside you not by a person but by God, it will prevent you from becoming something you are not meant to be. God told the Prophet Jeremiah this in the first chapter of the book of Jeremiah: *"before I formed you in the belly, I knew you... I ordained you to be a prophet to the nations."* Jeremiah had to choose to align himself with what God had chosen for him. When I faced alternative choices, I had to choose what God had selected for me.

This is the part where I had to let go of everything I felt I had built myself to be, the choices I made about who I was. However, holding on kept me from accessing the true legacy within me. Letting go of my past was a gradual, difficult process because it was deeply ingrained in me. It took a real-life shattering experience to break free. To illustrate, when Saul was riding to kill Christians, he was knocked off his horse and blinded by God. Immediately, Saul understood this was God's act, leading to his transformation from Saul to Paul. In this experience, his true legacy was unlocked — it wasn't to kill Christians but to spread the gospel of Christ. Similarly, when God literally knocked me off my horse of false humility, secret pride, and lust, that was when real transformation began.

Transformation for me was not pretty, but it was necessary. Moving from a life wrapped in shame and living ashamed to a life built on legacy happened privately, but its effects were visible to all. When I started to live a life of the legacy that has been revealed within me, that's when true legacy truly exists. Legacy resides inside a person, waiting to be uncovered. To you reading this, I want you to realize that legacy is calling you and waiting for you to partner with it. Legacy needs you to become a partner to bring it to life. Yes, I understand you may have other goals and plans, but I want you to remember that your genuine legacy must be uncovered within you and seen in you. If anything—whether a person, place, or thing—does not resemble what you've seen inside yourself, then don't connect with it.

I want to encourage everyone reading this that there is greatness within you! You have so much more to offer than you realize, so let this be the day your inner legacy is awakened. When I look back and reflect on my younger years, they were spent under what I was labeled as. As I mentioned earlier, because I stuttered, I was labeled because of that.

When I moved from Bushwick to Flatbush, I had to take a verbal test to determine my elementary school grade placement. During the test, I could hardly get the words out because of nervousness, and I was placed in the correct grade, but the class I was in was far below my academic level. I was labeled because of this, which led to a tracking system being established based on that label. As the school year went on, the teacher realized I was misplaced and incorrectly labeled. My teacher then called for me to be tested again, and this time the label was removed, replaced with a new one that also carried new responsibilities. Looking back, this new label also caused a shift in my academic trajectory.

Looking back on this, I realize that labels can create legacy, which can also bring shame to a person if they are ashamed of the label and legacy.

MAN IN THE MIRROR

Brian Bentley

I'll begin my story by introducing myself. My name is Brian. I was born and raised in a single-parent home with my little sister in Georgia.

My life was pretty good at first; we lived with my grandmother. You see, my grandmother was a devoted Christian. She introduced me to God. We attended church at least three times a week, and she maintained a Godly household. I was baptized at age six and was part of the church choir, enjoying life as God intended.

At that age, I didn't know much about God; I just knew what my grandmother told me about Him. My mother and grandmother had a big falling out; they were always arguing, and we had to find a new place to stay, so we moved to Atlanta.

We stayed in a shelter for a few months before getting our place in one of Atlanta's worst projects—Perry Homes. Once we arrived there, I knew life wouldn't be the same. Well, in the early 80s, my mother was addicted to crack cocaine. That's when life got tough. We hardly had any food in the house, no money, and no one to help us. My little sister and I were being teased about the old clothes we wore to school and how the kids mocked us because of my mother's addiction.

My sister and I always cried and prayed, hoping things would get better, but they never did. By the time I turned twelve, I was on the streets trying to make any money so my sister and I could have something to eat and wear new clothes to school. That's when I started selling drugs, stealing cars, and robbing people.

You see, the streets raised me. The men in my life were all about making money and having things, with the attitude, (I PAY THE COST TO BE THE BOSS!). These men taught me the morals of the streets—how to survive in the jungle with lions—so my thinking wasn't normal.

By the time I turned 15, I was in a gang, had been shot twice, and was making a lot of money at that point. I was building a reputation in my neighborhood. The guys I worked for started trusting me more, giving me new responsibilities. I felt good knowing I could take care of my family, even though my mother was still struggling with her addiction.

My sister and I weren't the jokes of the hood anymore. We had everything—new clothes and shoes. I bought my sister a new bicycle. I provided food for our house and ensured the bills were paid. I changed from Brian to BIG B. In my eyes, our life was almost back to normal—except for what my mother was going through.

And I want to let you know, I never stopped going to school. I was in 11th grade at age 15. I loved attending school to show off in front of the girls, and I still got good grades. The dealers I worked under ensured they'd give me money for good grades. It was a no-brainer to me—I could earn four or five hundred dollars just by going to school and doing what I needed to do. For me, it was all about the money, so it was never a problem. Things changed in the summer of '91. My best friend and I decided to go to the other side of Atlanta and steal some cars to sell to the chop shop for a couple of hundred dollars each.

Young guys from Georgia came up for the summer to work for him. Coming to New York was a new world for a country boy who had never been out of his home state.

During my first summer there, I experienced a lot, and the people around me taught me how to handle myself and hustle, make my own money, and live by my own rules.

By the end of that summer, I had saved enough and went back to Macon with all the drugs and the knowledge I needed to get this money. By 17, I had opened a weed spot and a crack house. I built a solid team of hustlers who looked out for each other, but more importantly, we shared the same passion — making money. For about two years, I thought things were going well. I had an apartment, two cars, many women, and plenty of money. I felt like a boss. No one could tell me anything; I was my own man. That's when I started selling guns in the city, and my cousin and I discovered there was a considerable demand for handguns. We knew we could get them cheap in Georgia, so that's what we did.

What we didn't realize was that we had been selling guns to an undercover cop for a year. It all ended in December 1999 when I was arrested on two counts of attempted murder and gun sales. I got into a shootout in Harlem when two guys tried to rob me of $60,000 and 40 pistols. I had to shoot my way out of a project building into the hands of the NYPD.

I thought my life was over—I'd never been in such serious trouble. The police had all the evidence against me. When I went to court three months later, I was offered thirty years to life. I felt like I was going to die.

When I returned to my cell on Rikers Island, I fell to my knees and started praying to God for help. It felt different because I hadn't done that in a long time—I had forgotten how to pray. I stayed on my knees almost all night, crying and asking God to help me and bring me out of this situation because He knew I deserved to be here.

I prayed earnestly every day for two years and began to change. I read my Bible more — it was the only way to soothe my mind and soul. It felt like God was speaking to me through memories of my grandmother when I sat alone in that dark cell. Her words hit me like bullets piercing my body and ripping through my soul.

I promised God that if He could bring me out of this, I would become a changed man, for Him and my family. I did something different each day to shift my thinking and ways. I believed God would free me from prison.

During those two years, my sentence remained the same every time I went to court. The district attorney wanted me to serve 30 years to life. But God had other plans. When it was over, I was offered ten years and accepted it, another blessing from God.

The moral of my story is how God brought me back to Him in my time of need. I am no longer the hustler or gangster I once thought I was in the mirror. Now I see a man of God who wants to live happily under God's mercy. I am still a work in progress.

THE EARLY YEARS
OF HIDDEN GRACE

Marvin Gross

Looking back on my childhood, I can still see myself sitting quietly in a corner of the house, eating mustard or jelly sandwiches, whispering, "When I grow up, I'll never eat like this again." Those words came from a place of longing for more food, more stability, and more love.

At that time, I thought I was forgotten and poor. I didn't realize that those simple meals, just mustard between two slices of bread, were God's way of providing for me and keeping me alive.

I didn't have much, but I had enough. And enough is where the lessons of my faith begin. I didn't realize back then that the adults raising me, my foster family, were doing the best they could. Their main focus was survival- making sure we had a roof, heat, and somewhere to sleep. My young mind couldn't understand the sacrifices behind that roof or the prayers that might have been said just to keep the lights on.

As I reflect on it through the lens of faith, I see what I couldn't see before: God was already providing. He was feeding me through hands that didn't even fully know Him. He was training my heart to find gratitude in small things so I could one day appreciate His greater blessings.

"The Lord is my shepherd, I shall not want." **Psalm 23:1**

"The eyes of all look to You, and You give them their food in due season." **Psalm 145:15**

"And my God will supply all your needs according to His riches in glory in Christ Jesus." **Philippians 4:19**

Like the Israelites in the wilderness, I was living on "manna," God's daily bread for survival. They complained because they wanted more, but that manna sustained them for forty years. I, too, didn't understand that God's enough is greater than man's plenty.

"Then the Lord said to Moses, 'Behold, I will rain bread from heaven for you; and the people shall go out and gather a certain quota every day." **Exodus 16:4**

"He humbled you, causing you to hunger and then feeding you with manna to teach you that man does not live by bread alone but by every word that proceeds from the mouth of the Lord." **Deuteronomy 8:3**

Even as a child, I longed to fit in to be like other kids. I didn't know I was different, or that the family I was in wasn't my biological family. I tried my hardest to please my mom, not realizing she wasn't my birth mother. I didn't know that I was in foster care. But now, as a man who's met Jesus, I see that God had already chosen me for adoption not by a family, but by His Kingdom.

"God sets the lonely in families." **Psalm 68:6**

*"Even if my father and mother abandon me, the Lord will take care of me." **Psalm 27:10***

"He predestined us for adoption to sonship through Jesus Christ, according to His pleasure and will."

Ephesians 1:5

Even in that house where I felt unwanted, God was writing my story. His provision wasn't just food and shelter; it was providence. Every hardship was shaping the person I would become. So, to anyone reading this who feels unseen or forgotten, let me remind you: God's provision isn't just what you hold, it's what keeps you. His hand has been on you even when you don't recognize it.

"The Lord will perfect that which concerns me."
Psalm 138:8

*"The Lord is good to those who wait for Him, to the soul who seeks Him." **Lamentations 3:25***

Protection: The Hidden Hand of God

I used to think protection meant being kept from pain, hardship, trials, and setbacks. But I've learned that sometimes protection means being kept through pain, surviving hardships, walking through trials, and overcoming setbacks.

Growing up, I was filled with anger. I didn't understand why I was treated the way I was. I remember one beating so clearly: I was hit in the eye with a belt buckle, and in a moment of fear and rage, I shouted, "You're going to kill me!" My foster mother responded coldly, "Then die."

That moment changed something in me. My heart grew cold. I began fighting back. I learned to numb myself to pain. I told myself, "If they can't break me, they can't hurt me."

What I didn't realize back then was that the real fight wasn't with my family, it was against the bitterness trying to take hold in my soul.

"For we wrestle not against flesh and blood, but against principalities, powers, rulers of darkness, and spiritual wickedness in high places." **Ephesians 6:12**

I thought I needed to protect myself, but God was already doing it. Every time I survived a beating, endured rejection, or stayed alive in situations that could have ended me, God was guarding me.

"The Lord will keep you from all evil; He will keep your life." **Psalm 121:7**

"The angel of the Lord encamps around those who fear Him and delivers them." **Psalm 34:7**

"When you pass through the waters, I will be with you; and through the rivers, they shall not overflow you."
Isaiah 43:2

When they locked me in a room and nailed the windows shut, I laughed at first, thinking, "They can't touch me now." But that laughter covered fear. I was trapped in that room and in my own rebellion.

Later, that same rebellion landed me in prison at seventeen years old. I was supposed to be playing college basketball. Temple and other schools were looking at me. But I was running the streets, caught up in anger, pride, and poor choices.

And yet, even there behind prison bars, God's protection didn't leave me.

"He will rescue you from every trap and protect you from deadly disease." **Psalm 91:3**

"No evil shall befall you, nor shall any plague come near your dwelling." **Psalm 91:10**

"For He shall give His angels charge over you, to keep you in all your ways." **Psalm 91:11**

I could have died in prison. I saw men lose their lives over pride, glance, and nothing at all. I saw hatred eat men alive from the inside out. But somehow, I made it through time after time.

When I faced a forty-year sentence for kidnapping and weapons charges, everything in nature said my life was over. Even my public defender didn't have hope. But I had something rising inside me, something I couldn't explain then.

It was faith and God's grace that turned the case around. I walked free. I was guilty of many things in my life, but that day, I learned what mercy truly meant.

"He who dwells in the secret place of the Most High shall abide under the shadow of the Almighty." **Psalm 91:1**

"The Lord will fight for you; you need only to be still." ***Exodus 14:14***

"You intended to harm me, but God intended it for good." **Genesis 50:20**

That was the beginning of my awakening. I realized that God had protected my body and my destiny. He covered me when I didn't deserve it. He hid me when I should've been exposed.

So now, when I think about protection, I don't picture bodyguards or walls, I picture grace.

"But the Lord is faithful; He will strengthen you and protect you from the evil one." 2 Thessalonians 3:3

"The Lord is my rock, my fortress and my deliverer."
Psalm 18:2

"You are my hiding place; You will protect me from trouble and surround me with songs of deliverance."
Psalm 32:7

Presence: The Power That Never Left

If provision sustained and protection preserved me, God's presence transformed me.

For much of my life, I didn't truly understand what it meant to walk with God. I believed He existed, but I didn't believe He was *near.* I thought He was distant, silent when I prayed, absent when I cried, and indifferent when I wandered. I imagined Him as a faraway deity, not a loving Father who longed for a relationship. But now I know the truth: He was there all along.

He was there when the lights went out and the darkness became my only companion.
He was there when I sat in a cold, lonely cell, wondering if life still held meaning.
He was there when rebellion filled my heart, when my words were laced with anger, when I pushed Him away in confusion and pain.

Through every mistake, every tear, every act of defiance, His presence never left me. He didn't rush away when I failed. He didn't withdraw when I turned my back. Instead, He waited patiently, lovingly guiding me toward the moment I would finally open my heart to Him.

"Where can I go from Your Spirit? Or where can I flee from Your presence? If I ascend into heaven, You are there; If I make my bed in hell, behold, You are there." **Psalm 139:7-8**

"Be strong and of good courage; do not be afraid, for the Lord your God is with you wherever you go." **Joshua 1:9**

"The Lord is near to all who call upon Him, to all who call upon Him in truth." **Psalm 145:18**

Something inside me changed when I met my best friend, the woman who introduced me to Jesus. I didn't realize it then, but God had sent her as a living example of His presence. She carried peace like a fragrance. She prayed with conviction, worshiped without hesitation, and loved people in a way that felt pure and unconditional. Through her, I began to catch a glimpse of what life in God's presence truly looks like.

At first, I went to church out of curiosity, not conviction. I didn't understand what drew me there; I only knew that something inside me changed when I walked through those doors. The heaviness lifted. The noise in my mind quieted. The ache in my chest eased. It wasn't the music or the sermon; God's presence washed over me, whispering, *"Welcome home."*

*"You make known to me the path of life; in Your presence there is fullness of joy; at Your right hand are pleasures forevermore." **Psalm 16:11***

*"The Lord replied, 'My Presence will go with you, and I will give you rest.'" **Exodus 33:14***

*"The Lord your God in your midst, the Mighty One, will save; He will rejoice over you with gladness." **Zephaniah 3:17***

God's presence didn't just transform my surroundings; it transformed my spirit. I started to view life differently. Conviction took the place of complacency. I ceased lying so easily. I stopped justifying sin with the excuse, "God knows my heart." I realized He wasn't looking for perfect behavior but longing for surrendered hearts.

His presence became my reflection, showing me not what I was, but what I could become in Him. It softened the hardened places, healed old wounds, and redefined what mattered most.

The presence of God teaches you to live differently, love more deeply, and forgive more freely. It shifts your perspective from *what you've lost* to *what He's redeeming*. It changes your definition of success from earthly applause to divine approval. It turns pain into purpose and bitterness into boldness.

"In all your ways acknowledge Him, and He shall direct your paths." **Proverbs 3:6**

"Draw near to God, and He will draw near to you." **James 4:8**

"Blessed are those who have learned to acclaim You, who walk in the light of Your presence, Lord." **Psalm 89:15**

I realize God's presence isn't limited to a church building or a Sunday morning service. It's more than just a moment; it's a way of *life.* It's the quiet confidence that He's already there, no matter where I am. It's waking up each day knowing I'm never walking alone.

When the path is uncertain, His presence steadies me. When storms arise, His presence surrounds me. When I'm weary, His presence renews me. And when I can't see my way forward, His presence becomes the light that leads me home.

"I am with you always, even to the end of the age." **Matthew 28:20**

"The Lord will guide you continually and satisfy your soul in drought." **Isaiah 58:11**

Now, I don't chase feelings or signs. I rest in the confidence that His presence is the greatest gift of all— the power that never leaves, the love that never fades, and the peace that surpasses all understanding.

Reflection: Living in His Presence

If you're reading this and wondering whether God is with you, let me tell you plainly: He is. Even when circumstances don't make sense and the future feels uncertain, His presence has not left you. He is closer than the very breath in your lungs, working in ways you may not yet see or understand.

You might be in a season of *lack*, but He's providing, maybe not always in the way you expected, but always in the way you need. You might be surrounded by *chaos*, but He's protecting and building a hedge of grace around your heart, keeping you grounded in His peace. You might *feel* alone, but He's present, whispering comfort and reminding you that you are never forgotten or forsaken.

"The righteous cry out, and the Lord hears them; He delivers them from all their troubles." **Psalm 34:17**

"Surely goodness and mercy shall follow me all the days of my life, and I will dwell in the house of the Lord forever." **Psalm 23:6**

When life breaks us open, God is not absent in our pain. He's there refining, reshaping, and restoring what was once shattered. God never wastes pain. Every hardship becomes a classroom of His faithfulness, a testimony waiting to be shared.

Your story may not look like mine, but His fingerprints are just as visible on your journey. Each trial has been a thread in the tapestry of His grace, woven together to reveal His goodness in time.

Remember this truth:
His provision nourishes you when you're empty.
His protection shields you when you're vulnerable.
And His presence changes you from the inside out.

Even in your quiet tears and silent prayers, He's shaping something beautiful around you and *within you*. Living in His presence isn't about perfection; it's about *trusting* that He is enough, *believing* that He is near, and *resting* in the assurance that His goodness will follow you all the days of your life.

A Closing Prayer for You

Father God,

Thank You for being my Provider when I had nothing, my Protector when I was in danger, and my ever-present help when I felt alone. Thank You for sustaining me through storms, for covering me with mercy, and for walking beside me in every season.

Help me to recognize Your hand in my life in the small things and the great things. Strengthen my faith to trust You more deeply, follow You more closely, and serve You more faithfully.

Let my story be a reflection of Your grace, so that others may come to know You as Provider, Protector, and Present Savior.

In Jesus' mighty name,

Amen.

BATTLE-TESTED

EARL CARPENTER, JR.

Ecclesiastes 1:9 states, "The thing that hath been, it is that which shall be and that which is done is that which shall be done: and there is nothing new under the sun". The last statement of this verse is extremely significant in shaping my understanding of life and the things I go through or am faced with. By stating that there is nothing new under the sun, the Prophet helps me realize that every temptation, every struggle, every obstacle, every addiction, and problem I have, or may face, has been experienced before. This is not meant to belittle anyone's issues, but it is a constant reminder that nothing I've ever experienced is new, and more importantly, that I have had help with every adversity I have faced in life. Our Savior, who took the form of flesh, experienced life as we live it and showed us, through His obedience and faith in God the Father, that we can overcome all things.

Luke 4:1-13 tells us that the Holy Spirit led Jesus into the wilderness, and after forty days of fasting, he was tempted by the devil three times. When Jesus was hungry, the devil suggested he should turn stones into bread. This was to get Jesus to show his power freely from God. Next, he showed Jesus all the world's kingdoms and offered Him power over all the world's kingdoms if He would worship him. He offered Jesus ill-gotten authority. And finally, the devil took Jesus to the highest point of the Temple and tempted Him to jump from the temple, claiming God's angels would protect Him.

Satan was tempting Jesus to test God's promises. In each case, Jesus resisted temptation by quoting scripture, demonstrating that we should live by God's word and that God alone is worthy of being worshipped and served. For me, this was a valuable life lesson.

I was a late bloomer. I accepted Jesus into my life at the age of 40. I have always thought of that as being late in life, and I am always grateful that the Lord kept me during a period when I deliberately chose not to follow Him. If there was ever an example of "Lord, if you just get me out of this, I swear...I would be the poster child for this. Whether by my own choices and devices or by circumstance, there were many times I have looked back at my life and easily identified times when the Lord brought me through or saved me from a situation.

In *John 15:16,* Jesus says, *"You did not choose me, but I chose you and appointed you that you should go and bear fruit and that your fruit should abide, so that whatever you ask the Father in my name, he may give it to you"*. Because of how I chose to live my early life, this verse is significant because, as previously stated, I constantly think about situations and circumstances in which God was with me even before I knew him. God chose me, even when I did not want to choose Him.

Why Am I Here?

Jeremiah 1:5 says, *"Before I formed you in the womb, I knew you; before you were born, I set you apart."*

One of the first things I learned when I got saved was that God has a purpose for me. He has placed me on this earth for a reason. With this understanding, I realized that I am on a mission. We all are. Whether we believe in Christ or not, we all have a purpose. So, what is my mission? I have no idea. But I don't need to know.

Isaiah 55:8-11 says, *"For my thoughts are not your thoughts, neither are your ways my ways, saith the LORD. For as the heavens are higher than the earth, so are my ways higher than your ways, and my thoughts than your thoughts. For as the rain cometh down, and the snow from heaven, and returneth not thither, but watereth the earth, and maketh it bring forth and bud, that it may give seed to the sower, and bread to the eater. So shall my word be that goes forth out of my mouth: it shall not return unto me void, but it shall accomplish that which I please, and it shall prosper in the thing whereto I sent it".*

The greatest revelation for me from this passage is that all I need to do is OBEY! Why obey? Because I understand that even if God sat me down and explained His plans to me and for me, my finite mind would not comprehend His plan. My

46

finite mind would not grasp the whys and hows of the things that have been or are yet to come. My small, limited mind would probably explode trying to grasp and/or understand where and why I fit into God's plan. And when I've gone through trials, would I have done so if I had known those trials in advance? What I have figured out is that if I try to live my life in accordance with His word and will, God will get out of me whatever fruit it is he has intended. Along the journey to accomplish my mission, I have been and will be tested, challenged, and impeded. Sometimes, these have been a result of my own actions or disobedience. Sometimes things were set up to cause me to stumble. Regardless of circumstance, throughout my life, I have been battle-tested. I am here today because I have not yet completed my mission. God still has work for me to do.

God's Work

Please walk with me so I can show you God's work and the battles I've won.

I was a 17-year-old senior in high school. The end of my senior year was approaching, and I was looking forward to graduation. I went to get fitted for my cap and gown and was told that my name was not on the list for graduation, and I needed to see my counselor. In discussion with my senior counselor, unbeknownst to me, I was informed that I had failed a class in the 10th grade that was mandatory for graduation. It was the last semester of the school year, just under a month before graduation, so it was too late for me to make up the class. I was told I must go to summer school or return next year to retake the class. I decided not to return the following year and did not finish high school. This decision led me to join the Army. It was a difficult decision because I had sworn I would never join the military. Vietnam had just ended a year before, and I had worked with some Vietnam vets who had set my mind against ever serving in the military. However, never say never!

Isaiah 42:16 says, *"and I will bring the blind by a way that they knew not; I will lead them in paths that they have not known: I will make darkness light before them, and crooked things straight. These things will I do unto them and not forsake them"*.

Let me be clear. I knew "of God" at this time, but I was at a point in my life where I had chosen not to want to know God. However, joining the Army led me to become the first in my family to earn a graduate degree. I also completed my undergraduate degree, graduating summa cum laude with a 3.9 GPA.

My graduate degree was an MS majoring in Strategic Intelligence with a minor in Latin American Studies, and I graduated with a 3.8 GPA. Considering how little I cared or thought about education when I was younger, I praise God for how that gradual, quiet change came about while I was in the Army.

I quickly learned the difference education would make for my military career and embraced it. I reached a point where I loved to learn and was at my happiest when researching and writing, whether at work or school.

God moved in me in a way that produced a side of me I didn't know I was capable of but came to embrace, love, and foster. In fact, when I accepted Jesus as my Lord and Savior, I studied God's Word with the same fervor as I did when I studied in school or wrote analytical papers for work.

I was blessed to be often recognized by my Pastor during Bible study, and he would ask me to lead Bible study when he was away on travel. My passion for studying God's Word also led to my Pastor trusting me to lead the training for new Deacons.

God brought this blind person in a way I did not know and led me down paths I had not known. The education I once did not value or appreciate when I was young has become a significant part of who and what I am today.

One way I view life today is that every day I learn something new is a good day, and I thank God I have many good days.

Battle-Tested

Psalm 32:8 says, *"I will instruct thee and teach thee in the way which thou shalt go: I will guide thee with mine eye."*

I joined the Army in March of 1977, served for more than twenty years, and absolutely treasured my time in the Army. I consider my entire career a huge continuous blessing. All my experiences, the travel, the things I learned, and the growth, all made me the person I am today. When I joined, I intended only to fulfill my four to six-year obligation. But of course, God had other plans. The totality of my military life had a tremendous effect on my life as it is today. There were so many experiences I recall, and only now understand that God was watching out for me the whole time. Allow me to share a few with you.

My first duty station was Germany, and I had a friend named James, who was my first mentor. James was nine years my senior, had served in Vietnam, spoke five languages, practiced martial arts, and was a wealth of knowledge and common sense, and he taught me so much about the Army and life in general. He was also one of the first people to see potential in me. One of the first and most important lessons I learned from James was that every assignment in the Army is what you make of it. Wherever I was, especially overseas, I needed to learn about my environment. Learn about the people, the language, and the culture, and make the best of it.

This is a lesson I have applied to life in general, and it helped me understand that while I could not control everything that happened to me, I could control how I responded.

The second thing was an actual introduction to religion. The first religion I actually studied was Taoism. James, my roommate Mike, and I used to spend hours on Saturday afternoons studying Tao Te Ching's text. The religious book *Tao Te Ching* is a collection of 81 prose or poems by Lao Tzu. The principal message of Taoism is to live in harmony with the Tao, or the natural flow of the universe, by embracing balance, moderation, and non-action (effortless action) while avoiding extremes, ego, and rigid desires.

By observing nature and cultivating inner stillness and self-awareness, one can surrender to the present moment, accept life's challenges with wisdom, and find true peace and effectiveness. Since this was the beginning of my military career, it was impactful in calming me and teaching me patience, which helped me navigate the craziness of military life without fighting the tide. I did not recognize it at the time, but meeting someone like James at the beginning of my career when I was so young and impressionable was truly God sent. He could have been a negative influence, but God sent me a stabilizing influence.

Isaiah 41:10 *Fear thou not; for I am with thee: be not dismayed; for I am thy God: I will strengthen thee; yea, I will* *help thee; yea, I will uphold thee with the right hand of my righteousness.*

As my second tour in Germany was coming to an end, so was my time in the Army. I was at a crossroads and had to decide whether I would leave the Army or re-enlist and continue my military service. I was honestly struck with fear because the decision would affect me and because I had a wife and son to care for. I did some research to figure out how my job, as a tactical radio operator, would translate to a civilian job. It did not. There were no civilian jobs that I could transfer my skills. Meaning, after eight years of military service, if I got out, I'd have to start all over in whatever career I could find as a civilian. Then, there were quite a few other incidents I could talk about from my time in the Army, but I want to take a moment to note two things of major importance that I constantly recall that let me know God has a mission for me.

First, between 1977 and 1997, the U.S. was involved in at least seven military operations or interventions. In twenty years of service, during which seven actions took place, I never spent one moment in a zone of conflict. I came close three times. In 1989 (Operation Just Cause), 1991 (Operation Desert Storm), and in 1995 (Operation Deliberate Force in Kosovo). On two of those occasions, I was on call to go, but combat operations ceased, and they stopped sending additional personnel. On the third occasion, in 1995, I got as close as being on an Albanian airbase, but I was still a considerable distance from any type of combat activity.

Twenty years of service, seven military operations, and God kept me away from any possibility of danger.

The second major event was the loss of my son. In August 1988, my four-month-old son passed away. I was stationed at Fort Meade, MD, but was away from home attending a leadership course at Fort Devens, MA. The course was a little more than three months long. We had finished the course and spent the last week completing administrative matters before graduation.

It was a Monday morning. My Sergeant Major called me into his office to inform me he had just received a call from the Red Cross giving notification of the death of my son. My son was four months and ten days old, and I had been absent for three months of his short life. Before I left for training, I was blessed to be able to spend a considerable amount of time with him every day the first month of his life because of my work schedule.

However, with his passing, I was never angry at God for taking my son away. I experienced considerable pain for the loss, but it never occurred to me to be mad at or blame God for this huge loss to my family. I never asked God why he did this. This happened well before I accepted Jesus as my Savior, and I did not belong to any religion. I had profound grief, and the pain was sometimes unbearable, but somewhere in my soul, I knew that there was a reason that my son was no longer with us, and if God decided that he needed him, it must have been a good one.

Hood, TX. I had previously spent two years there, and that place was the absolute worst duty station I had ever served, and without reservation the worst two years I spent in the Army. I can honestly say that in twenty years it was the only place I had been stationed that I hated, and I did not want to return to.

I was really worried about my next step because neither choice was a desirable one. However, once again, God provided, in a huge, totally life-altering way. I shared my fears with a coworker, and she suggested that I talk to the unit reenlistment counselor. She did not know how he could help, but she thought it could not hurt to talk to him.

I stopped by his office and explained my dilemma. Within minutes, he suggested that I change my career field. He described a program the Army had that I could go through to change my career field from the Signal Corps to Military Intelligence (MI). He also helped me find the best job I could transition into under MI that would not be such a drastic change from what I was currently doing.

This move was absolutely life-changing, and because of this new career, I stayed in the Army. I absolutely loved my new job and was very successful. Every assignment brought new, exciting, and diverse experiences and growth that were rewarding both professionally and personally, and resulted in a highly decorated career. It was also a job that seamlessly transferred to civilian life. There were quite a few other incidents I could talk about from my time in the Army, but I want to take a moment to note two things of major importance that I constantly recall that let me know God has a mission for me.

First, between 1977 and 1997, the U.S. was involved in at least seven military operations or interventions. In twenty years of service, during which seven actions took place, I never spent one moment in a zone of conflict. I came close three times. In 1989 (Operation Just Cause), 1991 (Operation Desert Storm), and in 1995 (Operation Deliberate Force in Kosovo). On two of those occasions, I was on call to go, but combat operations ceased, and they stopped sending additional personnel. On the third occasion, in 1995, I got as close as being on an Albanian airbase, but I was still a considerable distance from any type of combat activity. Twenty years of service, seven military operations, and God kept me away from any possibility of danger.

The second major event was the loss of my son. In August 1988, my four-month-old son passed away. I was stationed at Ft Meade, MD, but was away from home attending a leadership course at Ft Devens, MA. The course was a little more than three months long. We had finished the course and were spending the last week completing administrative matters before graduation. It was a Monday morning. My Sergeant Major called me into his office to inform me he had just received a call from the Red Cross giving notification of the death of my son. My son was four months and ten days old, and I had been absent for three months of his short life.

Before I left for training, I was blessed to spend a considerable amount of time with him every day the first month of his life because of my work schedule. However, with his passing, I was never angry at God for taking my son away. I experienced considerable pain for the loss, but it never occurred to me to be mad at or blame God for this huge loss to my family. I never asked God why he did this. This happened well before I accepted Jesus as my Savior, and I did not belong to any religion. I had profound grief, and the pain was sometimes unbearable, but somewhere in my soul I knew that there was a reason that my son was no longer with us and if God decided that he needed him, it must have been a good one.

Preparing to retire from Army, once again renewed fear arose because I was starting over. Again, God did not let me go. Despite my lack of diligence in searching for employment, I got a job through a friend who had retired a month before me, and I didn't miss a paycheck.

My first paycheck from my new job came two weeks after my retirement from the Army. Within five years of retiring from the Army, I finished my BS degree, got a job in the federal government, and most meaningfully, I came to my senses and accepted Christ as my Lord and Savior. Again, God favored me. This time, not just with a good supervisor but with another mentor.

My new boss taught me so much. He admittedly hired me because of my varied experience in inter-agency relationships and broad experience and knowledge of the intelligence community. He hired me for a job which I had no experience, but he felt I had good management skills, and that he could teach me the rest. The most profound thing he ever told me was that I was "teachable".

He said, with as good as I had been with so many things, I never acted like I knew everything, I was not afraid to ask questions or refuse assistance or guidance. That was something that stuck with me.

In **Isaiah 41:10,** God says, *"Fear thou not; for I am with thee: be not dismayed; for I am thy God: I will strengthen thee; yea, I will help thee; yea, I will uphold thee with the right hand of my righteousness".* I flourished in my twenty years in the federal government, holding managerial and supervisory positions with great responsibilities, and almost every job dealt with inter-agency relationships, which ended up being my specialty.

I worked for a Department of Defense agency that supported the warfighter, and I was still subject to deployment to a combat area even as a civilian. As with my military career, I never served in a dangerous area during my twenty years of federal government service. Don't misunderstand, I did deploy. In fact, between 2009 and 2015, I was deployed four times. But even with four deployments in six years, I was never in a combat area. There was one occasion when I was scheduled to deploy to Afghanistan. Still, during the final exercise of our training, when I jumped from the second floor of a building during a live-fire exercise, I severely twisted my ankle. This happened two weeks before my deployment date, and with my ankle in a cast, I was unable to deploy because of the injury. Painful though it may have been, once again, God kept me out of harm's way.

I have been retired for four years now. I often tell my wife that I frequently look back over my life and am convinced that God was with me, even before I knew or wanted to know Him.

As I mentioned before, I came to God later in life, but my understanding of who He is and my past experiences have led me to believe that the Lord has a specific purpose for me. I served twenty years in the Army, another twenty years in the federal government, and I have survived prostate cancer twice. I do not know what that purpose is, but that doesn't matter.

What matters is that, with the Holy Spirit guiding me and Jesus interceding for me, God has carried me through many trials. The fact that He continues to wake me daily indicates that my purpose is not yet fulfilled. My wife and I live a very comfortable life, a life I asked the Lord to bless me with

When I was younger, I told the Lord I never wanted to be rich; I just wanted to live without struggling to get by or living paycheck to paycheck. And that is exactly the life we have now. The Lord provides for us to enjoy the things we want without hardship. One of my granddaughters says, "Sometimes life is lifing." I have found that to be very true.

Life has given me many turns, tests, and trials, but when God has a mission for you, I've learned to trust Him because He will see you through every battle. In my retirement, I am blessed beyond measure. God has provided me with everything I have asked for and everything I could want. A life that I truly do not want for anything, and I am totally grateful for everything.

There is a song called "Thank You" by The Wardlaw Brothers that causes me to tear up when I hear it because it mirrors my life. It describes the feeling of going through life and dealing with struggles and failures, but understanding and acknowledging that God is always there, giving me strength, forgiveness, blessings, and love despite my failures, mistakes, and shortcomings.

God held me when I felt like giving up, He picked me up when I fell, and He constantly shows me He loves me. I just want to say thank you, Lord!

THE REBUILD

REGINALD LANDRUM

There was a time when I thought I had everything figured out. I had my plans, path, and pride neatly lined up. Marriage, work, success — the things I thought defined a man. But somewhere along the way, I realized I wasn't building according to God's blueprint. I was building according to my plan.

When life started crumbling, I tried to patch it up with my strength. I could fix it if I worked harder, loved stronger, or hustled longer. But I didn't realize then that God can't bless who we pretend to be. He blesses the man who surrenders.

It took divorce, prison, and losing everything I thought made me a man to show me that I was never meant to live by my own design — I was meant to live by His design.

It all started in 2010, when I was officially divorced in June. At the time, I looked at it as if I was free to do what I wanted after a six-year relationship and ten-year marriage. But I was sadly mistaken. I got into one relationship after the next, and one of my girlfriends actually told me she had a dream of me going to prison. I quickly rebuked that in the name of Jesus. A lot of the time, God gives us forewarning, but we don't take heed.

The Bible says in **_Jeremiah 29:11_**, _"For I know the plans I have for you, declares the Lord, plans to prosper you_ *and not to harm you, plans to give you a hope and a future."* I used to quote that verse without truly understanding it. But when you've lost it all — your marriage, your freedom, your livelihood — that Scripture becomes more than words. It becomes oxygen.

Looking back, I can see that God wasn't punishing me. He was positioning me. Every piece that broke had to break, because He was rebuilding me into something new — not the man I thought I was supposed to be, but the man He always designed me to become.

When I Hit the Wall

My defining moment didn't come with a bright light or a booming voice from Heaven. It came in silence — in a cell, surrounded by regret.

Prison was never part of my plan. It wasn't even a detour I could have imagined. Yet there I was, stripped of everything — my name, pride, and freedom. Divorce had already cut deep, but prison cut to the bone. I had failed as a husband, a father, and a man. The enemy whispered, "You're done. God can't use you now."

But in that darkness, God spoke louder than the lies. It wasn't with words at first; it was with presence. There's something about being broken before God that opens your spirit to His voice. ***Psalm 34:18*** says, *"The Lord is close to the brokenhearted and saves those who are crushed in spirit."* That verse became my lifeline.

I remember sitting on the cold concrete floor one night, praying not for release but restoration. I didn't ask God to take me out — I asked Him to come in. And He did. In that stillness, He reminded me that my worth wasn't in what I had done, but in who He was.

That was the night I realized I couldn't rebuild myself. I had tried everything in my power to get released, but nothing worked. I needed the Master Builder. God showed me that even the ruins of my life could become the foundation for something new — if I let Him design it.

That defining moment wasn't about escape. It was about encounter. It was about meeting Jesus not at the top of my success, but in the ashes of my failure. When I realized that I had to let go and let God things started to click. I was able to release anger and forgive people who wronged me. I even forgave the person responsible for me being there, Me. I blamed the person who gave information to the federal government for a long time but ultimately I was to blame, so I forgave Reggie.

Isaiah 61:3 says He gives *"beauty for ashes, the oil of joy for mourning, the garment of praise for the spirit of*

heaviness." I was living proof that His word still works —
even behind bars. Through it all I was able to finally have a
Relationship with God and I even started my Comedy career
in there doing the joke of the day. I said if I can make
prisoners laugh, I can make anyone laugh.

Rebuilding My Identity, Character, and Calling

When I walked out of those walls, I thought freedom
meant I was finally "back." But real freedom wasn't about
walking out — it was about walking with Him.

The first thing God rebuilt was my identity. For years, I
thought being a man meant being strong, self-sufficient, and
in control. But God showed me that real strength is in
surrender. My identity wasn't in my past, possessions, or
position. It was in Christ.

2 Corinthians 5:17 says, *"If any man be in Christ, he is
a new creature; old things are passed away; behold, all things
are become new."* That verse wasn't a nice thought — it was
my truth.

He also rebuilt my character. Prison teaches patience.
Divorce teaches humility. Job loss teaches dependence. God
used every season to shape my heart. He taught me to listen
more than I speak, to love without conditions, and to lead by
example, not ego.

I used to measure success by status. Now, I measure it by obedience. He stripped away my pride so He could reveal my purpose, which is witnessing to young men and getting them back into the kingdom!

Then came the calling. I discovered that my pain had a purpose — to help others rebuild their lives. God gave me what I call the "gift of helps." I find joy in repairing what's broken, not just physically, but spiritually. Whether it's encouraging a brother who's lost his way or helping someone get back on their feet, I see now that God was preparing me for this all along.

James 1:2-4 says, *"Consider it pure joy, my brothers, whenever you face trials of many kinds, because you know that the testing of your faith produces perseverance."* My trials weren't wasted. They were training.

Unlearning the Lies

Before I could walk in truth, I had to unlearn the lies.

The first lie was: *"You're disqualified."*
The truth: *Romans 8:1* says, *"There is therefore now no condemnation to them which are in Christ Jesus."* God doesn't throw away broken men — He restores them.

The second lie was: *"It's too late."*

The truth: **Philippians 1:6** reminds me, *"He who began a good work in you will carry it on to completion."* God doesn't stop building just because we hit rock bottom. In fact, He often starts there.

The third lie was: *"Real men don't cry."*

That one took a while. But I've learned that tears don't make you weak — they make you real. Even Jesus wept. Strength isn't the absence of emotion; it's the presence of faith in the middle of it.

And finally, I had to unlearn: "God can't use me." That's one of the enemy's favorite lies. But if God can use Moses after murder, David after adultery, and Peter after denial, He can surely use a man like me.

The truth set me free — not just from prison walls, but from mental and spiritual chains. **John 8:32** says, *"You shall know the truth, and the truth shall free you."*

Living by His Design Now

Today, I live differently. I live by His design.

I don't chase success anymore; I chase purpose. I don't live for approval; I live for alignment. Every day I wake up with a mission — to help men rebuild.

I work with my hands, but I lead with my heart. God's given me opportunities to speak into the lives of men who are walking through the same valleys I once crawled through. I tell them the same thing God told me: You are not done. You are being rebuilt.

When I face challenges now, I remind myself of **Ephesians 2:10**: *"For we are His workmanship, created in Christ Jesus for good works, which God prepared in advance for us to do."* That word "workmanship" means masterpiece. Even when I don't see it, God is still shaping me.

I no longer see my past as shame — I see it as soil. The very ground that once buried me now grows my testimony.

God's design for my life is simple: to walk in truth, serve with humility, and love without limits. I'm still a work in progress, but now I know whose hands I'm in.

A Word to the Next Generation of Men

Brothers, if you hear nothing else, God still builds men.

This world will tell you your worth is in your wallet, job, or relationships. But those things can vanish overnight. Authentic manhood isn't about what you have — it's about who you belong to.

If you've been through a divorce, you're not damaged goods. If you've been to prison, you're not disqualified. If you've lost your job, you're not worthless. Those are not your endings — they're invitations for God to start something new.

Be careful not to confuse activity with purpose. Just because you're busy doesn't mean you're building. Let God be your architect. Surrender your blueprints.

Don't isolate yourself. Find brothers who will hold you accountable, pray with you, and remind you who you are in Christ. And that is precisely what we have been doing every Saturday at 8:30 AM. By His Design men's fellowship because men need an outlet and somewhere to speak, be heard, and be healed. Amen, the enemy loves lonely men because lonely men are easy to lie to.

And to the young men coming behind us — don't wait until life falls apart to seek God. Seek Him now. Build on the Rock while you have the chance.

1 Corinthians 16:13-14 says, *"Be watchful, stand firm in the faith, act like men, be strong. Let all that you do be done in love."* Strength without love is just control. But strength with love — that's power under submission.

Micah 6:8 sums it up: *"He has shown you, O man, what is good. And what does the Lord require of you? To act justly, love mercy, and walk humbly with your God."*

That's what living by His design looks like. It's not flashy. It's faithful. It's not about perfection — it's about persistence.

Closing Reflection

If I could sum up my story in one sentence, it would be this:
God didn't rebuild me to restore my past; He rebuilt me to release my purpose.

Divorce broke me. Prison humbled me. Losing my job stripped me. But grace — grace rebuilt me.

And now, when I look in the mirror, I don't see the man I used to be. I know the man He always meant for me to become.

So, if you're standing in the rubble of your life right now, don't lose hope. The same God who raised Jesus from the dead can rebuild you, too.

Let Him draw the plans. Let Him set the foundation. Let Him be your design. Because what's built by His hands — stands.

KINGDOM MANHOOD

REGINALD GANT

The Crisis of Modern Masculinity

We currently live in a time when masculinity is both under attack and misunderstood. Cultural narratives about what it means to be a man are often distorted because they are usually driven by media, shifting moral standards, and conflicting expectations. Some men feel pressured to still embrace the "tough guy" persona, shutting down emotions and dominating others, while other men are encouraged to abandon traditional leadership roles altogether. Simply put, they're just passive and unavailable mentally and emotionally.

In the middle of all this chaos and confusion, God's Word provides clarity. Before culture even had a "voice" or influence, God designed manhood with deliberate intention and purpose. The blueprint for masculinity was set in motion in the Garden of Eden, and it has never changed. Even when Adam fell, the layout for real masculinity was still in play.

I can recall a season in my life when I was a young college student attending the illustrious Morgan State University. It was the first time that I had freedom and autonomy. However, it was also the first time so many other females surrounded me. Growing up in Baltimore City, I was familiar with our women, but on campus, there were beautiful girls from Washington, DC, PG County, Philly, New York, down south, the west coast, and even many more from overseas and other continents. At that time in my younger life, because of the culture and influences of media and entertainment, I thought that masculinity meant that I had to chase and conquer as many girls as possible. And honestly, that was my goal. However, I would later come to realize that this was never God's original definition of manhood.

God's Original Blueprint for Manhood

When God created Adam, He established the foundation for manhood. Adam was given responsibility, identity, and authority. He was not appointed to exploit, but to serve, protect, and steward. In *Genesis 2:15*, God placed Adam in the garden to work it and take care of it. This reveals that manhood, since inception, was rooted in responsibility and stewardship.

Although my younger days were filled with partying and chasing women, I quickly began to realize that something was missing. The conviction that I felt when I would do certain things outside of God's way of living always weighed heavily on my heart. The more I learned about Christ and His word, the more messed up I saw my life. Oftentimes, I was extremely distant from the man that God had created me to be, so the battle between being what culture defined as a man and what God intended was always a tug of war for me. I am certain that many men can relate.

It wasn't until I settled down and got married that I truly began to realize and understand what being a real man was.

True manhood means being responsible for yourself and your actions, properly leading others toward Christ, and becoming the optimal version of yourself. And, how do you do that? You lead by example. You go the way and show the way first. This not only pleases God, but it has always been our purpose as men. I would even venture to say that getting married is the best decision that a man can ever make if he is marrying the woman that God has created for him. Why? Because it is through marriage and parenting that you really understand who you are, as both reflect a mirror pointing back to you. They point to you as a leader, as an example, and as the head. You can literally witness your fruit right before your very eyes, and many men are not willing to endure such a tough and tumultuous assignment. So, many men, oftentimes, quit and/or walk away. Or even worse, they remain, but live in a watered-down and weak version of manhood that God never intended.

The Counterfeit Masculinity Trap

The enemy has worked tirelessly to distort God's design for manhood. He uses various tricks, schemes, plots, and tactics. As men, we take the bait for so many of them. For some, it's the trap of aggression and dominance; for others, it's passivity and neglect. Both extremes miss the mark of God's original intent for manhood. Men were never created to display aggression and dominate women, however, this current culture seems to celebrate and validate those traits. In the Garden of Eden, God provided all that Adam and Eve needed. They had safety, provisions, and most importantly, they had God. And God is love. So, when love is present, there is no need or room for aggression.

Jesus Christ then came along and modeled a better way for men. He came and displayed such characteristics as strength under control, power rooted in love, and authority expressed through service. Alas, real and authentic manhood. True manhood. Manhood God's way. This was always the manhood that was to be modeled. However, the media and culture's voice have drowned out the true voice of God. And, if we are not careful, it will continue to do so for generations to come.

I remember one time when I was having a conversation with a married neighbor. He was talking about women, chasing skirts, and carrying on. He hinted at the fact of cheating and stepping outside of his marriage a few times, and then he asked me, "You know what I mean. You know what it's like, right?". I seized this opportunity and moment quickly by standing up for my Christian values and principles. I told my neighbor that I never believed in cheating or stepping outside of marriage because that is called adultery. I shared a verse that mentioned how the sins of the father are passed down to the third and fourth generations *(Exodus 20:5)*. At that moment, I stood up for what was right and for my beliefs and values. I used that opportunity with him to share how I overcame the cultural lies about manhood. Not all men cheat despite what culture says. Many actually love their wives and are committed to their wives and families. And to wrap up this story quickly, would you believe that he never mentioned anything about cheating ever again? From then on, he only talked about how much he "loved" his wife. Men, sometimes we have to be the ones to stand up and be the voice of what real manhood is. We must be the model for all to see. This world desperately needs our example.

Kingdom Manhood Defined

Up until now, we have discussed the crisis of modern masculinity, God's original blueprint for manhood, and the counterfeit masculinity trap that many men fall into headfirst. It's time we park for a moment and actually lay out and define what true, authentic Kingdom Manhood really is. A Kingdom man is a man who places himself under the rule of God and aligns his life with Kingdom principles. His identity is not shaped by trends, cultures, influences, or traditions of this world, but by the truth of Scripture. A Kingdom man is rooted in and uses the word of God as his book of instruction for wisdom and guidance.

A Kingdom man seeks first the Kingdom of God and His righteousness *(Matthew 6:33),* and he leads with humility, courage, and love. These three powerful characteristics are at the core of every godly man. Is he humble? Has he displayed courageous behavior (standing up for what is right, what is fair, and what God says in His word) even in the face of adversity? Does he walk and operate in love?

Being married to an amazing wife and raising five children (four sons who are still at home with us) is no easy task. It is not for the weak or faint of heart by any means. As demanding as it can be, there are still rewards that I will never be able to put into words. In my house, Sundays are for church, but it didn't start that way, if I could be honest. When I left the church I was attending to explore the church that my wife was attending, it was a challenge for me at the onset. I was used to a traditional church where service was in the morning, so I was home by afternoon for football. For many men, we know that football or sports is their Sunday god, but that's another conversation for another time. *Identity* crisis?!

My wife and her church worshipped at 2 pm because they were renting space from another church while they were raising funds for their very own building. Let's be clear: a service starting at 2 pm meant that I was missing not only major parts of the 1 pm football games but also cut into the 4 or 4:30 games on the back end. I was not happy at all in that season. Can you tell what god I was serving? I was making football my god when, instead, it should have always been about the God who woke me up and blessed me to be and have all that I am and have.

As our family started to grow, and we had more sons, I realized that they would model and do what I say and did. If I didn't take them to church, they would deem that as a way of life and possibly not take their future wives and children to church. If I drank alcohol and smoked, more than likely, they would feel free to do the same. So, I had a decision to make. And, it was a tough one then, but it is no longer tough at all now. I decided that I would model and demonstrate to my wife and sons that our kingdom values are always priority even above and over personal comfort. Even on the Sunday's when I am not feeling it, I am transparent in telling my sons, and my wife, that real manhood is about sacrificing for the greater good. Just because I may not feel like attending church service doesn't negate the fact that we should still attend as a family.

Who am I to rob or deny my loved ones of a word or an encounter that may have been just for them because of my selfishness? So I love the fact that I can be free and transparent because I am now leading my family the right way. There can be grace given when I fall because they see and know that the true intention is living life God's way even when I mess that up and fail. Kingdom manhood is and has always been about humility (sitting your pride down), courage (doing what is right because it is right), and love (demonstrating love God's way).

Practical Pillars of Kingdom Manhood

When it comes to Kingdom Manhood, what we are anchored in matters. Let's discuss five practical pillars for Kingdom Manhood. I love the word pillar because its meaning is a person or thing regarded as reliable and providing essential support for something. You don't think your way in or stumble into kingdom manhood. It is intentional. It requires effort. The foundation must be firm. Here are the five pillars:

Spiritual Leadership. Kingdom Men should lead in their homes, workplaces, businesses, and community. They should be doing this through prayer, utilizing the word of God, and by leading by example.

Stewardship. Kingdom Men are called to manage resources, time, and talents as servants of God. Understand and know that everything is His and for His purpose. Therefore, steward all accordingly. Nothing should be wasted. Nothing underutilized.

Courage - Kingdom Men stand for truth, even when unpopular. They know that the culture and all its influence will be against them, but they remain ten toes down on God's word, nonetheless. In all we do as Kingdom Men, we should always be pointing others back to Christ. And that requires courage.

Integrity – Kingdom Men live with consistency between their private life and public life. Who they are when no one is watching should match and reflect who they are when the world is paying close attention. Many men are living a double life, and scripture records that a double-minded man is unstable in ALL of his ways.

Servant Leadership – Kingdom Men use their position to elevate others, and not themselves. In Mark 10, it is recorded that even the Son of Man came not to be served, but to serve. Kingdom Men give back. They roll up their sleeves and pitch in. They do not neglect the things of God, but more importantly, they do not neglect the needs in their very own homes first. Home is where true servant leadership begins.

With the honor and privilege of raising four young men, integrity is extremely important to me. My wife and I are teaching our sons all about character and integrity. Who you are when no one is watching matters. Being a person of your word matters. Operating in excellence matters. Our sons are starting to understand, but I can see the internal struggle with our teenage son right now.

Torn between his middle/high school years and trying to identify where he fits in, combatted with all the various social media platforms and their distractions, bumped up against all the word that he hears in church on Sunday are a lot for anyone to take in. I am starting to notice his discomfort because he feels that he has to be one way around his "friends" and another way around his family. I take time to remind him that consistency is key. Authenticity is where it's at. Being who you are everywhere you find yourself is powerful.

There is freedom in being who you are and who God designed you to be. But, he's a teen. Think back to your teenage years when your parents tried to guide you down the right path. How many times did you look at them like they were ancient and take another way instead? So, knowing this, I live a life of integrity for him to model, and I trust that he is in God's hands. This is real masculinity. I will never encourage him or any other male to be anything or anyone other than what God has created them to be. I just wish that men would have done the same for me when I was growing up. But, since that did not happen, now it is time that I (and you) pay it forward.

Living Beyond Culture's Definition

Culture demands that manhood is about power, possessions, and prestige. How many men can we look to in our time and see that they have abused all three of these? I do not have to name any names, but many have risen and fallen, some have served time in jail because of it, and others have even committed the ultimate act of suicide. Why? They had what culture defined as "success", but they lacked the ways and mind of God to sustain it.

The Kingdom, however, says that true, authentic manhood, God's way, is all about purpose, purity, and perseverance. To live beyond culture's definition, you must renew your mind daily with the word of God *(Romans 12:2).*

I can recall a time in life when I used to cut corners. I would take shortcuts and do things in a less-than-excellent manner. That included how I filed taxes, what I put into my body (alcohol), and even the words that came from my mouth (profanity). And then I got married. Men who marry me truly make all the difference because that woman has the power and ability to elevate us to higher heights or bring us down to the pits of mediocrity and subpar living.

Having the godly wife I am blessed to have, I was called up to a higher standard. She did not lie or cheat, so I stopped. She did not drink alcohol of any kind or form, so eventually I stopped. She did not use aggressive language or profanity either, so I stopped as well. The world wants men to believe it is all about power, prestige, and possession, but that is far from the truth. Kingdom Manhood is about identifying and walking in our God-given purpose. Being pure before The Father as best as you can. Kingdom Manhood is about your ability to persevere at all costs, even amid challenges and adversity, because you know you have a God who fights for, defends, and protects you. We no longer live by the definition of manhood that culture dictates; instead, we rise above it. And, we teach others to do the same. Low-level living is behind us now. Kingdom Men RISE UP.

The Ongoing Journey

Kingdom manhood is not a one-time achievement. It's a lifelong pursuit. The closer you walk with God, the more He reveals new areas for growth, and the more responsibility He entrusts to you. To whom much is given, much is required.

Philippians 3:14 says, *"Press on toward the goal for the prize of the upward call of God in Christ Jesus"*. The Apostle Paul knew that pressing on was essential. We discussed perseverance earlier, and the ability to forge ahead no matter what. The same is true for us.

At this current phase of my life, I am now locked in. I am committed. I understand that God is teaching me more and more daily that I was (and we all are) made in His image. My marriage should reflect Christ. Yours should also. The works of my hands should reflect Christ. Yours should also. The words I use and the way I live my life publicly and privately should reflect Christ. Yours should also.

As a Kingdom Man, I now understand that I have the power, influence, and authority to impact and shift the culture. And, with this awareness and mandate, I boldly walk in who I am because I know whose I am. Kingdom Manhood is truly living beyond the culture's definition of masculinity. We are the light and the model for the world to see.

Closing Charge & Prayer

The world is desperate for men who will reject passivity, embrace responsibility, lead courageously, and invest eternally. Your family needs you. Your community needs you. The Kingdom needs you. Are you willing to stand up for what really matters? Are you ready to lay down your way of living and pick up the mantle of living that Jesus demonstrated for us in the Bible? Authentic Kingdom Manhood.

This isn't about living a life of perfection because none of us will ever be perfect. However, it is about direction. Decide, day after day, to align your life with the Word of God, and let His Spirit shape you into the man that you were created, destined, and purposed to be.

My Prayer

Father, I thank You for every man (and woman) reading these words. Thank You for designing these men with purpose before they ever drew their first breath. Lord, I pray that You would break every chain of counterfeit masculinity in their lives. Remove the lies of culture and replace them with the truth of Your Word. Fill these men with the courage to stand firm, humility to serve, and love to lead well. Strengthen their hands for the work ahead and guard their hearts against distraction. Let their lives be a reflection of Your Kingdom and a testimony to Your goodness. In Jesus' name I pray, Amen.

Now, go forth and conquer, king!

FROM HUSTLER TO STEWARD

EMANUEL OWENS

I didn't become a hustler because I was evil. I became one because I was afraid.

I grew up in church, but when pressure hit—pressure to provide, escape poverty, and prove I was a man—I reached for the hustle. Culture told me manhood was about performance, possessions, and staying ahead, so I made money my measuring stick. If I could grind harder than the next man, stay guarded, stack cash, and never show weakness, I believed I would finally feel secure.

But success without purpose is just survival dressed up.

I said I was "providing," but I was building my kingdom. The hustle owned me. I was working nonstop, anxious, always chasing the next level, but never satisfied. Then God interrupted me and showed me something I didn't want to admit: He never called me to hustle. He called me to steward.

The Illusion of Control

The world keeps telling men to "secure the bag," "build the brand," and "protect the image." So, we chase money, opportunities, and status, and tell ourselves this is leadership. What we don't see is that much of that drive is fueled by fear—fear of failure, fear of lack, and fear of being exposed as "not enough." Hustle can produce temporary gain, but it can also steal deep peace. I had resources, but I didn't have rest. I

thought I was in control, but I was actually being controlled—
by pride, by pressure, and by a false definition of masculinity.

We cling to control because we want certainty. We don't
like unknown outcomes, so we act as if everything depends on
us. Our minds look for patterns, even in random events,
because we would rather believe that our choices always
determine results than admit that grace and God's sovereignty
are involved. And sometimes it's just ego—we would rather
say "I did this" than "God did this." That kind of control can
motivate us, but it can also blind us and push us toward risky
decisions and constant disappointment when life doesn't obey
our plans. Real manhood is not rooted in control; it is rooted
in surrender. God didn't create men to be slaves to the grind
but managers of His gifts.

The Breaking Point

Eventually, there came a moment when everything I was
building started to crumble. Finances tightened. Relationships
became strained. Purpose felt blurry. I realized I had built on
sand and called it success. That is where God met me. He did
not meet me with condemnation but with clarity: "Son, I didn't
call you to hustle. I called you to be a steward." That single
word shifted everything. It meant I was not the owner—God
was. It meant I was supposed to live under His authority, not
my ambition. It reminded me of Job, who lost wealth, health,

and family, not because God didn't love him, but because God was revealing what his faith was truly built on *(Job 1-2)*.

God often uses two kinds of seasons to form us. In seasons of testing, He allows loss, betrayal, or disappointment to reveal whether our trust is in Him or in what we've built *(1 Peter 1:6-7)*. In seasons of personal failure, He lets us discover that our strength, discipline, and good intentions are not enough to sustain faithfulness. Both kinds of seasons are meant to humble us, detach us from earthly security, and prepare us for a greater calling.

What Stewardship Really Is

Stewardship isn't just about money or church giving. It is a way of living before God. Paul wrote, *"Now it is required that those who have been given a trust must prove faithful"* *(1 Corinthians 4:2)*. That means everything I have is something I will one day answer for. The starting point is ownership: God owns everything— *"The earth is the Lord's, and everything in it" (Psalm 24:1)*. If He owns it, then my role is not to possess but to manage. From there flows responsibility: I am called to use, protect, and grow what He has placed in my hands. After that comes accountability: like the servants in *Matthew 25:14-30*, I will one day give an account for how I handled His resources, opportunities, relationships, and influence. And finally, there is reward: faithful stewardship leads to blessing in this life and in the next.

When I lived like a hustler, I acted as if everything belonged to me. I worked from fear. I gave because I felt obligated. I made plans without prayer. When I shifted to stewardship, I realized God was not trying to take from me; He was trying to involve me. He was inviting me out of survival and into significance.

Money with a Mission

One of the first areas God restructured in me was money. I stopped seeing money as proof of my worth and started seeing it as a tool for God's Kingdom. ***Proverbs 3:9*** says, *"Honor the Lord with your wealth, with the first fruits of all your crops."* That verse taught me two things at once: God goes first, and generosity is worship. I began to tithe with joy rather than fear. I gave not only to my church but to people in need. I started budgeting—not to shrink my lifestyle but to align my spending with my calling. I didn't chase money anymore; I told money where to go.

Money itself is not evil. Scripture is clear that it is the love of money that is the root of all kinds of evil (1 Timothy 6:10). Hustling often trains us to love money more than mission. Stewardship trains us to make money serve the mission instead of replacing it.

Redeeming Time and Talent

Money wasn't the only thing I mishandled. I had also mismanaged time and buried talent. I had gifts, but I wasted years trying to impress people. Then God reminded me, *"We are God's handiwork, created in Christ Jesus to do good works...which God prepared in advance for us to do". (Ephesians 2:10).* God didn't just save me; He assigned me.

As a steward, I began to ask different questions. I asked whether I was using my time to build what actually matters or just to maintain an image. I asked whether I was serving others with my gifts or simply promoting myself. I asked whether my schedule was prayed over or just packed. When I gave God my time and talent, He multiplied the impact. I stopped being busy and started being fruitful. I stopped being exhausted and started being aligned.

Redeeming time, as Paul says in *Ephesians 5:15–16*, means buying it back from waste, distraction, and sin and investing it in what matters eternally. Redeeming talent means refusing to let God-given skills, creativity, wisdom, and influence stay trapped in self-serving goals. Time is limited—once a day is gone, it does not return. Talent is God-given—like the servants with the talents in *Matthew 25*, we are expected to develop what He entrusts. Both time and talent are stewardship issues because we do not own either; we only manage them.

Leading from Surrender

Manhood is not about dominance; it is about responsibility. A Kingdom man doesn't lead by force but by submission to God first. As I embraced stewardship, I saw that real leadership meant covering, protecting, and guiding those God had entrusted to me. In practical terms, that meant praying with my family, listening before solving, taking responsibility for my mistakes, and choosing humility over ego. My old hustler self, wanted to control and impress. My new steward self wants to serve and bless.

Scripture is full of leaders whose authority came from surrender. Moses, David, and Paul were not powerful because they were flawless; they were powerful because they yielded. Surrender aligns a man with a higher authority so that he is no longer leading out of his own wisdom but out of God's direction. Worldly leadership says, "Prove yourself and stay on top." Kingdom leadership says, "Die to yourself and serve." Jesus modeled this perfectly—He emptied Himself and became the servant of all *(Philippians 2:7)*. Paul even said, *"When I am weak, then I am strong" (2 Corinthians 12:10)*, showing that God's power is most visible when we stop pretending to be self-sufficient. When a man surrenders his agenda, he becomes free to embrace God's mission. That keeps him from chasing titles, applause, or positions. He can lead with purpose, even when it costs him.

The Blessing of Alignment

When I embraced stewardship, I began to experience something I hadn't felt in years: peace. Not because my circumstances were perfect, but because I was finally in order. I trusted God with provision, I rested in His timing, and I obeyed what He said. *Matthew 6:33* became my anchor: *"Seek first the kingdom of God and his righteousness, and all these things will be added to you."*

I often think of alignment like a car. When the wheels are aligned, the ride is smooth, and the wear is minimal. When they are out of alignment, the vehicle fights you, drifts, and takes on unnecessary damage. Spiritual alignment works the same way. When your priorities, values, and purpose line up with who God says you are, your life moves with less friction.

The blessings of alignment are real. God gives peace—an inner calm and stability, even when life is chaotic *(Isaiah 26:3)*. He releases provision—resources flow more freely when we are in His order *(Philippians 4:19)*. He brings clarity—His voice becomes easier to discern. He grants favor—doors open, relationships appear, and opportunities come that we could not have manufactured *(Psalm 5:12)*. He gives protection—we stay under His covering and are spared some attacks and traps *(Psalm 91)*. And He produces fruitfulness—our work starts producing results that actually last *(John 15:5)*. Alignment, then, is not just avoiding sin; it is walking so closely with God that His power, provision, and purpose can move unhindered in our lives.

A Word to the Man Still Hustling

If you're still grinding, I understand. You want to provide. You want to win. You want to protect your name and the people you love. Those are good desires. But the hustle that is draining you is not the path God designed for you. What I learned is simple: God's provision is better than man's performance. Your identity is not tied to your income. You are not what you produce; you are who God says you are. Rest is not laziness; it is worship. Real men are not the ones who control everything—they are the ones who surrender everything.

So, lead from surrender, not pride. Don't mistake control for leadership. Pride will destroy you faster than failure ever will. Yielding to God will make you stronger than competing with everyone around you. Guard your character more than your reputation, because reputation is what people see, but character is what God sees—and what you build in secret will eventually show up in public. Be faithful with the small things—your word, your money, your time—because if you can't manage those, you won't be trusted with more. Every man will wrestle with lust, greed, and pride; the key is to crucify them daily. What you refuse to put on the cross will one day try to put you on one.

Give It Back to God

This is the moment to pause and ask hard questions. What areas of your life are you still trying to control that God is asking you to surrender? What resources, relationships, or opportunities have you been holding onto as if you were the owner instead of the manager? Are you building your own kingdom, or are you managing His? Today can be the day you move from hustler to steward. God's blueprint for manhood is not about chasing more; it is about becoming more— through Him.

A Steward's Prayer

Father, forgive me for the times I hustled without You. I surrender every gift, every dollar, and every plan to You. Teach me to manage well what You have given me. Help me to lead with integrity, to give with joy, and to live with purpose. Make me a faithful steward of Your resources, Your people, and Your call. In Jesus' name, amen.

Scriptures for Meditation

Read and reflect on these passages slowly. *1 Corinthians 4:2* reminds us that anyone entrusted with something must prove faithful. *Proverbs 3:9* calls us to honor The Lord with our wealth. *Matthew 6:33* tells us to seek first the Kingdom of God and trust Him with the rest. Deuteronomy 8:18 reminds us that it is God who gives us the power to get wealth so that He may establish His covenant. *1 Timothy 6:10* warns us that loving money will lead us into trouble. *Ephesians 2:10* declares that we were created to do the good works God prepared for us long before we saw them.

Reflection

Think back to the moment when the hustle failed you. Was there a loss, a setback, or a spiritual encounter that exposed what you were really trusting in? How did you feel when God met you there—convicted, humbled, relieved, seen? Now consider stewardship. If God is the owner and you are the manager, how should that change the way you budget, serve, lead, and rest? Are you living for livelihood or for legacy? Are you using your gifts for a platform or for God's purpose? Jesus asked, *"What good is it for someone to gain the whole world, yet forfeit their soul?" (Matthew 16:26)*. That is the question every former hustler must answer.

Let God redefine your manhood. Not a hustler. **Steward.**

THE BLUEPRINT OF
A MAN

Eric Carpenter

From an early age, I grew up with an awareness of God. My parents ensured that we were in church, and as children, we were introduced to the routines of worship and community. They sent us to church. As we grew older, that awareness shifted into religious duty. We went to church because it was expected. I ushered on third Sundays and played basketball with my brother and uncles on the others. Yet, even in these moments of routine, God was near, though I did not fully understand His presence or His purpose for my life.

Looking back, I now see that God's hand was on me even when I didn't recognize it. Like many, I believed that as long as I was present in church, I was doing my part. But Jesus reminds us in **Matthew 15:**8, *"These people honor me with their lips, but their hearts are far from me."* My presence in the building did not always mean my heart was surrendered to Him. I knew of Him, but I did not truly know Him or seek His will for my life. I was out here just living. I am sure so many can relate.

As I grew older, I began making choices without consulting God. I joined the United States Army, eager to serve my country, and even graduated from high school early. Later, I married young without fully understanding the weight of the covenant I had entered. Like many men, I pursued life with zeal but little wisdom, making mistakes and decisions that carried consequences I could not easily escape. Still, even in those moments, God's grace was present. **Romans 5:8** reminds us, *"But God shows his love for us in that while we were still sinners, Christ died for us."*

In my failures, I discovered God's faithfulness. He looked beyond my faults and saw my needs. The same God who created me in His image **(Genesis 1:27)** did not abandon me when I strayed from His design. Instead, He used my experiences, both the triumphs and the mistakes, to shape me into the man He intended me to be.

Rediscovering identity in God's image means understanding that who I am is not defined by my failures, achievements, or upbringing, but by the eternal truth that I bear His likeness. Paul reminds us in *2 Corinthians 5:17*, *"Therefore, if anyone is in Christ, he is a new creation. The old has passed away; behold, the new has come."*

The blueprint of a man, then, is found not in culture, career, or even family expectations, but in God alone. My life's journey has shown me that His plan is greater than my mistakes, and His grace is sufficient to redeem every chapter of my story.

A Father's Example

My father played a vital role in shaping my early manhood. Though my parents separated and reconciled several times, my dad was consistent in his involvement. He may not have been perfect, but he was present. His presence mattered because it gave me stability in moments when life felt uncertain. He disciplined us firmly, sometimes with a heavy hand, but always with the intent of guiding us away from destructive choices. He reminded us often that life is about choices and that every choice carries consequences.

He instilled in us the importance of integrity, respect, and hard work. My father lived by the principle that a man's word should mean something. If you said you were going to do it, you did it. He also taught us to respect ourselves and others, no matter their position or status. These lessons mirrored biblical wisdom. *Proverbs 10:9* says, *"Whoever walks in integrity walks securely, but he who makes his ways crooked will be found out."* My father may not have quoted that scripture to us directly, but he lived it out in practical ways that made a lasting impression.

Another lesson my father drilled into us was the importance of staying out of trouble. He would warn us of the dangers of crime, careless living, and bad company. He made sure we understood that one wrong decision could alter the course of our lives. At the time, it felt more like fear than wisdom, but as I grew older, I realized he was teaching us to *"abstain from every form of evil"* (**1 Thessalonians 5:22**). His warnings became guardrails that kept me from traveling down paths that could have destroyed my future.

What stands out the most, however, is that his discipline and example gave me boundaries. Boundaries are often misunderstood as restrictions, but they are really protections. They help define where safety lies. In many ways, my father's presence and instruction created a hedge of protection around me, reminding me of the truth in **Proverbs 22:6**, *"Train up a child in the way he should go; even when he is old he will not depart from it."* Even when I strayed, the lessons I had been taught pulled me back toward center.

Still, while my father provided boundaries, it was God's unseen hand that ultimately gave me direction. My father could teach me how to live right, but only God could reveal His purpose for my life. **Jeremiah 10:23** declares, *"I know, Lord, that our lives are not our own. We are not able to plan our own course."* That scripture became real to me as I looked back and saw how God guided me even when I did not acknowledge Him.

In truth, my father helped shape the man I became, but it was God who shaped the man I was meant to be. My father laid the foundation of discipline, but God laid the foundation of destiny. Together, both influences remind me that the blueprint of a man is not just learned at home but discovered in the heart of God.

A Defining Moment in My Father's Life

My parents ultimately decided to divorce, and though that was a painful season, it became the turning point in my father's life. During that time of brokenness, my dad truly met the Lord. He had always believed in God on some level, but this time it was different he encountered Him for real. The change was undeniable. He started going to church, and it was there that he met Momma Jean. Together, they began a new journey, and I witnessed my father transform into the man of God he was always called to be.

There was something about the change in him that could not be denied. His walk changed. His talk changed. He was no longer the same man who had raised me with discipline and strong principles; now, his strength was anchored in Christ. *2 Corinthians 5:17* says, *"Therefore, if anyone is in Christ, he is a new creation. The old has passed away; behold, the new has come."* That scripture came alive in my father's life. The man who once relied on his own willpower was now led by the Spirit of God.

He married Momma Jean, and together they became a powerful example of faith and perseverance. My dad went from being a churchgoer to being a servant in the house of God. He became a Deacon and, in time, the Head Deacon at New Birth Missionary Baptist Church in Northeast Washington, D.C. He wasn't just filling a role, he was living a testimony. He taught Sunday School and led Bible Study, pouring into others the same discipline and integrity he had once poured into me, but now with a spiritual foundation that pointed back to Christ.

During those years, I was serving in different countries with the U.S. Army, but every time I came home, I noticed more changes in him. He had grown closer to God in ways that humbled and inspired me. He radiated peace, purpose, and wisdom. I was proud of him, not just as my father but as a man of God. His transformation showed me firsthand that no matter where life takes us, no matter how many mistakes we make or detours we take, God can still redeem and restore.

I remember visiting his church and being amazed at how respected he was, not because of titles or achievements, but because of the life he lived and the faith he demonstrated. **Proverbs 20:7** declares, *"The righteous man walks in his integrity; his children are blessed after him."* I was one of those children. His new walk blessed me, even as I wrestled with my own journey.

105

When I eventually returned and settled back in America, my own life began to take different turns. My marriage was unraveling despite our efforts to hold it together. My wife was a believer, and we had a beautiful daughter together, but somehow, we grew apart. What started as subtle distance became division, and ultimately, our marriage ended in divorce.

In the midst of my failures and the weight of poor decisions, I lost my marriage and found myself living in my brother's basement. It was a humbling season. At that time, my brother had already shifted his priorities. He had stopped playing basketball on Sundays and was faithfully going to church with his family. I never told him, but his quiet example was the first spark that inspired me to consider a different path and truly seek after God.

I began attending my father's church, where he was serving faithfully as Head Deacon. After only a few weeks, I was asked to serve as an usher. Not long after that, they invited me to join the choir, and within a few more months, the pastor asked me to serve as a trustee. It became clear to me that God had a plan for my life.

After about a year of living with my brother, I met someone through a coworker...a cousin who was a minister at her church. She began praying with me and for me. We started studying the Bible together and attending different church events, and once again, I could see God's hand at work. He was orchestrating every connection, every opportunity, because He knew the man I was becoming and that I couldn't make this journey alone. Yes, God had a plan, and He was patiently shaping me into it.

Watching my father's transformation in the same season I was facing brokenness reminded me that God is able to redeem any story. His life stood as a witness that it is never too late for God to take hold of a man and make him new. What God did for my father became a reminder that He could do the same for me. To understand our purpose, we must seek the creator God. His blueprint is the Bible.

God's Blueprint for Men

So, what is God's design for men? Scripture gives us a clear and powerful picture. From the very beginning, God had a blueprint for manhood, and His Word outlines the qualities that define who a man is called to be.

1. Identity as Image-Bearers

Genesis 1:27 declares, *"So God created man in his own image, in the image of God he created him; male and female he created them."* At the very core of manhood is identity. A man's worth is not defined by culture, status, success, or even failure; it is rooted in being an image-bearer of God. True manhood begins with knowing that we reflect His character, creativity, and purpose. This is why we are vital in our homes. As we bear His image and character, we can help our families to do so as well.

2. Leaders in Love and Servanthood

God designed men to lead, but leadership in His design is not about control or domination...it is about sacrificial love. *Ephesians 5:23* reminds us that *"the husband is the head of the wife as Christ is the head of the church,"* while verse 25 commands, *"Husbands, love your wives, as Christ loved the church and gave himself up for her."* Biblical leadership is rooted in service, humility, and sacrifice. The blueprint of a man calls for leadership that mirrors Christ. Leading not by power, but by love.

3. Workers and Stewards

From the garden of Eden, God established work as part of man's purpose: *"The Lord God took the man and put him in the Garden of Eden to work it and take care of it"* (*Genesis 2:15*). Work is not a curse but a calling. Men are designed to build, provide, and protect...not just physically, but also spiritually and emotionally. Stewardship means caring for what God has entrusted to us our families, our communities, and our callings.

4. Anchored in Faith and Integrity

Proverbs 20:7 declares, *"The righteous man walks in his integrity; his children are blessed after him."* A man's life is not measured only by what he accomplishes but by the legacy he leaves behind. God's design calls men to be spiritual anchors, teaching God's Word, modeling faith, and walking in integrity. Like my father, who grew into his role as a spiritual leader in his church and family, men are called to stand as examples that point others to Christ.

5. Strength Through God's Spirit

The Apostle Paul exhorts men in *1 Corinthians 16:13-14*: *"Be watchful, stand firm in the faith, act like men, be strong. Let all that you do be done in love."* True strength is not measured by physical might or personal pride but by reliance on the Spirit of God. Strength in God's design is always balanced with love.

6. Redeemed and Restored in Christ

Above all, the blueprint points us to Christ, the perfect Man. In Him, every broken piece of our story can be made whole. *2 Corinthians 5:17* reminds us, *"Therefore, if anyone is in Christ, he is a new creation. The old has passed away; behold, the new has come."* My father's transformation and my own journey both testify that no man is too far gone, no mistake too great, and no story too broken for God to redeem.

By His design, men are called to reflect God's image, lead with humility, serve with love, work with integrity, and anchor their families and communities in faith. This is not a cultural ideal or a man-made definition; it is God's eternal blueprint.

The blueprint of a man is not written by culture, mistakes, or even success. It is written by the hand of God. And when men align with God's design, they do more than build their own lives; they build legacies, families, and communities that stand strong on the foundation of Christ.

This is a tall order! But we are not alone. God calls us and equips us. Everything He requires of us, He helps us to do. He is my helper. Men, we must get in our Word. We must fellowship with other men on the same path of becoming who God called us to be. We must rely on God to help us as we worship and spend time in prayer. We must ask for forgiveness when we fall short and offer ourselves grace, too. I wish I could say this is easy, but it is not. I started worshipping with my dad, sitting at the feet of great men I admire and who reflect the image of God. I met my now wife, and she helped me change and get to know God personally for myself. We prayed together and did Bible studies together, and we still do. Those are the same things I do twenty-five years later. It's a decision that you must continue to make daily.

By His Design is a ministry that is a safe place for men to glean from one another. Bishop Rufus Mahon is one of my mentors. I attribute a lot of who I am today to my father-in-love, Bishop Easton Grant; my father, Deacon Earl Carpenter Senior; and my brother, Deacon Earl Carpenter Junior. I am grateful for a community of great men.

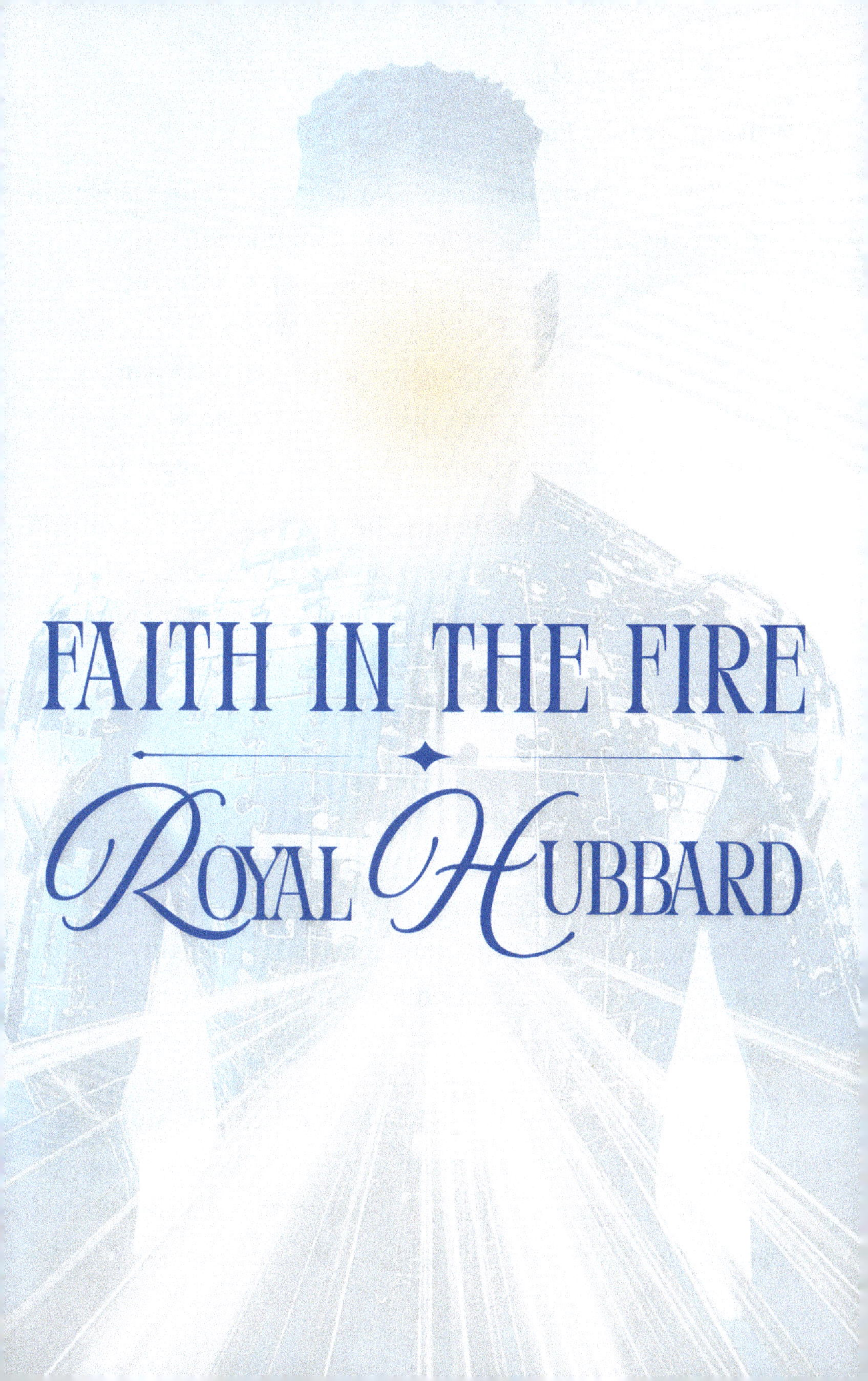
FAITH IN THE FIRE
ROYAL HUBBARD

Walking Into the Fire

The day my father died—November 1, 1989—is etched into my memory. I was fourteen, standing on the edge of childhood and manhood, and the one man I looked up to was gone. My father wasn't just a parent; he was my compass. Saturday mornings spent tagging along while he worked on property management jobs weren't just chores—they were lessons in responsibility, problem-solving, and integrity.

I remember that before he died, we were baptized together. I know now that I set my path in motion. When he died, the house was full—my mother, my three sisters, relatives—but I felt alone. Anger, grief, and a sense of abandonment burned through me like fire. I didn't run toward God. I ran toward the streets.

The streets called to me like a magnet. They promised belonging, excitement, and recognition. The flashy cars, the shiny chains, the way women smiled at the young men who had power—these were the images I thought defined manhood. At sixteen, I chased that image relentlessly.

Fire of the Streets

By sixteen, I was caught up in drugs and stolen cars, cycling in and out of jail. Every arrest felt like a punch to the chest, but I kept going back. I believed that if I just worked harder, hustled smarter, I could control the chaos. I didn't see

114

it at the time, but the streets were a fire, promising warmth but leaving me hollow inside.

I remember nights sitting on a stoop, cold wind biting my face, and wondering why I felt empty despite all the "success" the streets offered. I had the jewelry, the girls, the money—but inside, I was starving. I had lost my father, my role model, my guide. And I was trying to fill that hole with things that could never satisfy my soul.

The Rikers Fire

April 15, 1992. Locked up for drugs again, I found myself on Rikers Island, C74.

Rikers has a smell you never forget—a mix of sweat, metal, and despair. Doors slam constantly, voices echo, tension hangs thick in the air. I remember lying on my bunk at night, staring at the ceiling, and thinking: Is this my life? Is this my end?

God answered through a friend who told me about a program called JCap. "They'll come to court for you," he said. I called. They came. The judge released me into their care. My friend, the one who gave me the information, was denied. That was God's hand, right in the fire.

Walking into J-Cap for the first time, I was skeptical. I thought this was just another stop along my way. But then I started listening—truly listening—to the stories around me.

115

Stories of abuse, neglect, addiction, and loss. I realized I was addicted too, not to substances, but to the lifestyle, the money, the power. I was addicted to pretending I was in control.

Facing My Reflection at J-Cap

The program was small, just six other young adults. At first, I felt out of place. But then the director took notice of me. She gave me a leadership role called Young Adult Coordinator. I organized trips, outings, and activities. I could have walked away, but I didn't. That trust refined me, showing me the value of accountability and perseverance.

One day, I asked her if I could work outside the program. She agreed. I became a messenger in the city, responsible for packages and time-sensitive deliveries. No one else in the program had this opportunity, yet I was trusted. That responsibility was a fire—it demanded focus, discipline, and integrity. Every evening, I returned to the program and was reminded of the consequences if I strayed.

I saw something change in myself. For the first time, I understood that trust was a gift, not something to be taken for granted. The fire of accountability shaped me, teaching me lessons no street or jail cell could.

The Test That Almost Broke Me

GED classes were required, and then I discovered something incredible: I could attend college while working on

116

my GED. Sullivan County Community College offered a Hospitality Management program that felt right in my spirit.

I convinced the program to let me and a friend take the entrance exam. My friend went first and passed. I went second. I failed math. I remember sitting there, staring at the paper, feeling the weight of disappointment press down. My heart sank. God, how could You put this dream in me and let me fail? I felt like quitting. But my friend said, "I'm not going if you're not going." Faith was walking beside me, reminding me that perseverance is not a solo journey.

Two weeks later, I returned. My hands shook as I picked up the pencil. This time, I passed. The fire had tested my faith—not just my knowledge, but my willingness to keep going. I realized that failure isn't a stop sign; it's a signal to keep moving forward, to trust God even when the road is hard.

Discovering the Gift

Sullivan County became a sanctuary. Cooking revealed a talent I didn't know I had. The kitchen became a place of peace, creativity, and reflection. The fire hadn't destroyed me—it had refined me, revealing gifts I wouldn't have discovered otherwise.

I remember standing over the stove, mixing ingredients, tasting sauces, and thinking: This is joy. This is purpose. Every chop of the knife, every simmering pot was a reminder that

God's hand had been guiding me all along, even when I thought I was lost.

Faith and the Mind

The fire isn't just around you—it's inside your mind. When my father died, I felt abandoned. When I failed the test, I felt inadequate. When I sat in Rikers, I felt forgotten. That's where the enemy attacks hardest, planting doubt in the furnace of your mind.

Faith and doubt cannot coexist. Whichever you feed will grow. I learned to pray through the fear, to study scripture even when it didn't make sense, to meditate on past victories— even small ones. Each act of faith was like a brick in the foundation of a stronger me.

Remaining Steadfast

Being steadfast doesn't mean never feeling weak. It means refusing to let go of God when everything shakes. When I failed, I tried again. When I felt unworthy, I trusted anyway. Steadfastness isn't about my strength—it's about God's.

Every morning, I choose to stand. Every decision became a test of faith. And every step forward, no matter how small, reminded me that perseverance through fire builds character, resilience, and a deep, unshakeable trust in God.

Coming Out As Gold

Every fire had a purpose:

- Losing my father taught me I needed my Heavenly Father.
- The streets exposed the emptiness of false identity.
- Rikers forced me to seek another way.
- J-Cap refined me through trust and accountability.
- Failing and passing the test taught perseverance.
- Cooking revealed gifts hidden in ashes.

Job 23:10 says: *"But He knows the way that I take; when He has tested me, I will come forth as gold."* Every fire shaped me. None destroyed me.

After all the trials through my life, I ultimately found myself in the same career field my father was in—property management. It felt like a full-circle moment, as if God had been guiding me toward the skills and gifts my father had shown me as a boy. The hands-on expertise, the managerial insight, and the sense of responsibility I inherited from him became tools to serve others, and to honor his legacy.

I came out of the fire with a deeper understanding of life, a clearer sense of purpose, and a strengthened faith that no circumstance could shake.

Reflection for the Reader

- What fires in your life feel overwhelming?
- Can you see God's hand in seasons of loss or struggle?
- What gifts might He be refining in you right now?
- How can you remain steadfast even when the outcome is uncertain?

Conclusion: Refined for Purpose

Looking back over my life, I see a thread I didn't notice while living it. From my father's death, to the streets, to Rikers, to J-Cap, to discovering my passion, God was walking with me through every fire.

Here's What I've Learned:

- The fire doesn't mean God has left you. Sometimes it's proof that He is shaping you.
- Faith is not about seeing. It's trusting when you can't see the way out.
- Steadfastness is a daily choice. You stand again and again, even when weary.
- Your gifts are often hidden in ashes. Trials bring them to light.

Every reader is either in a fire, coming out of one, or heading into one. That's life. But the fire is purposeful. Every tear, every test, every challenge is allowed so you can come forth refined.

I started as a boy chasing an illusion of manhood. Today, I stand as a man who knows true strength comes not from status or possessions, but from the God who carries you through every season.

Faith in the fire is never wasted. God is not just watching—you are being worked in. Remain steadfast. Hold on. When the flames die down, you'll see that the fire didn't destroy you—it revealed who you really are.

MY PLAN, GOD'S PURPOSE

—— ◆ ——

BISHOP
PHILLIP CRICHLOW

Israel was in a hard season when Jeremiah wrote to them. They were far from home, living under a foreign power, and probably wondered, *"Has God forgotten us?"* Into that ache the prophet delivered a word from the Lord:

"For I know the thoughts that I think toward you, saith the LORD, thoughts of peace, and not of evil, to give you an expected end." **Jeremiah 29:11**

That letter was God's way of saying, *"I still see you. I still have a plan. Exile is not the end of your story."* And the same God who did not forget Israel has not forgotten you. He cannot. He says, *"Yea, I have graven thee upon the palms of my hands"* (**Isaiah 49:16**). A God who writes your name on His hands is not a God who loses track of you.

God Never Misplaces His Children

Sometimes believers feel abandoned—praying and nothing seems to move, serving and nothing seems to change. But our feelings are not always telling us the truth. The Lord is *all-seeing* and *all-knowing*:

"O LORD, thou hast searched me, and known me. Thou knowest my downsitting and mine uprising, thou understandest my thought afar off." **Psalm 139:1–2**

Because He knows us so well, He also knows how much we can bear. That's why Peter tells us: *"Casting all your care upon him; for he careth for you."* **1 Peter 5:7**

The enemy would love to whisper, *"God isn't with you...you don't deserve His love...you messed up too much."* But that's a lie. God's Word answers it: *"I will never leave thee, nor forsake thee." **Hebrews 13:5*** If God says *never*, He means *never.*

When God Interrupted My Plans

There was a season in my life when I didn't know who to call and didn't know what to do. On the outside, I was doing well. I had traveled and played drums with some of the greatest gospel singers and groups—the Mighty Clouds of Joy, the Blind Boys of Alabama, JJ Fadry, the Soul Stirrers, and with my own group, The Ecstatistics (my favorite!).

By many people's measure, I had "made it." I was working with legends. Doors were opening. However, success is not the same as purpose.

One day, while I was in New Orleans, I heard the Lord speak so clearly to my heart: *"I have given you everything you asked for. What are you going to do for Me?"*

At first I was stunned. *Me?* I knew my flaws. I knew my sins. I knew where I had fallen short. I thought, *"Surely God is talking to somebody else."* But He wasn't. He was talking to me.

And that's how God works. He doesn't call us because we are perfect; He calls us because He is. Paul said it like this:

"And I thank Christ Jesus our Lord, who hath enabled me, for that he counted me faithful, putting me into the ministry." 1 Timothy 1:12

God wanted to use me—for His purpose and His glory. That moment in New Orleans was the beginning of my real surrender. My plans had taken me far, but God's purpose was calling me deeper.

Discipled Into Purpose

After that, the Lord led me to Bishop James Eugene Berry. That connection was divine. Through Bishop Berry, God began to shape me. He didn't just tell me I had a gift—he taught me to build a real relationship with my heavenly Father. He said, *"You are called. You are chosen. You will preach the gospel."*

That didn't happen overnight. It took years of training, teaching, and studying the Word. But that is how God does it. He forms us before He fully releases us. Like Paul told Timothy, ministry is something you "continue in" *(2 Timothy 3:14)*. I kept growing. I'm *still* growing. I'm still becoming—

- a better pastor,

- a better husband,

- a better father,

- and, yes, the best grandfather I can be—so God gets glory from my life.

Looking back, I can see it so clearly: God's purpose for me was far greater than any plan I had for myself. Paul said, *"Now unto him that is able to do exceeding abundantly above all that we ask or think..."* **Ephesians 3:20**

That's my testimony. He went beyond what I asked. He went beyond what I thought. And I am grateful.

Your Turn

Now I want to speak to **you**, the one reading this chapter.

You are **not** forgotten.

You are **not** disqualified.

You are **not** too late.

Just as God spoke to Israel in Babylon, He is speaking to you in your season:

"For I know the thoughts that I think toward you..."
Jeremiah 29:11

God has a thought about you. Not a random thought—a good thought. A plan. A purpose. A future.

Maybe, like me, you don't feel worthy. Maybe you think, *"I've done too much wrong...God won't use me."* Hear this: God never makes mistakes. If He reached for you, it's because He wants you. Jesus said,

*"Ye have not chosen me, but I have chosen you, and ordained you, that ye should go and bring forth fruit..." **John 15:16***

That means you're chosen on purpose and for purpose. And part of that purpose is to be a witness—to tell every man, woman, boy, and girl that Jesus saves and that salvation is free to all who will receive Him and turn from their sins. (***Romans 10:9-10, 13***).

Let God Have His Way

Keith "Wonder Boy" Johnson sang, *"You ought to let go and let God have His way!"* That's really what this chapter is about. Surrender. Laying down *your* plan so you can walk in *His* purpose.

Because here's the truth:

*"And we know that all things work together for good to them that love God, to them who are the called according to his purpose." **Romans 8:28***

God works *all things*—the good, the bad, the confusing, the years in Babylon, the years on the road, the years you didn't know who to call—into purpose. So today, let His purpose begin in you.

A Prayer to Step Into God's Purpose

Father, in the name of Jesus,

Thank You for not forgetting me.

Thank You, that Your thoughts toward me are good.

I surrender my plans to You.

Use me for Your glory.

Heal what is broken, restore what is missing,

and lead me into the purpose You designed for me

before the foundation of the world.

I believe You will never leave me nor forsake me.

In Jesus' name, amen.

Now...let go and let God have His way.

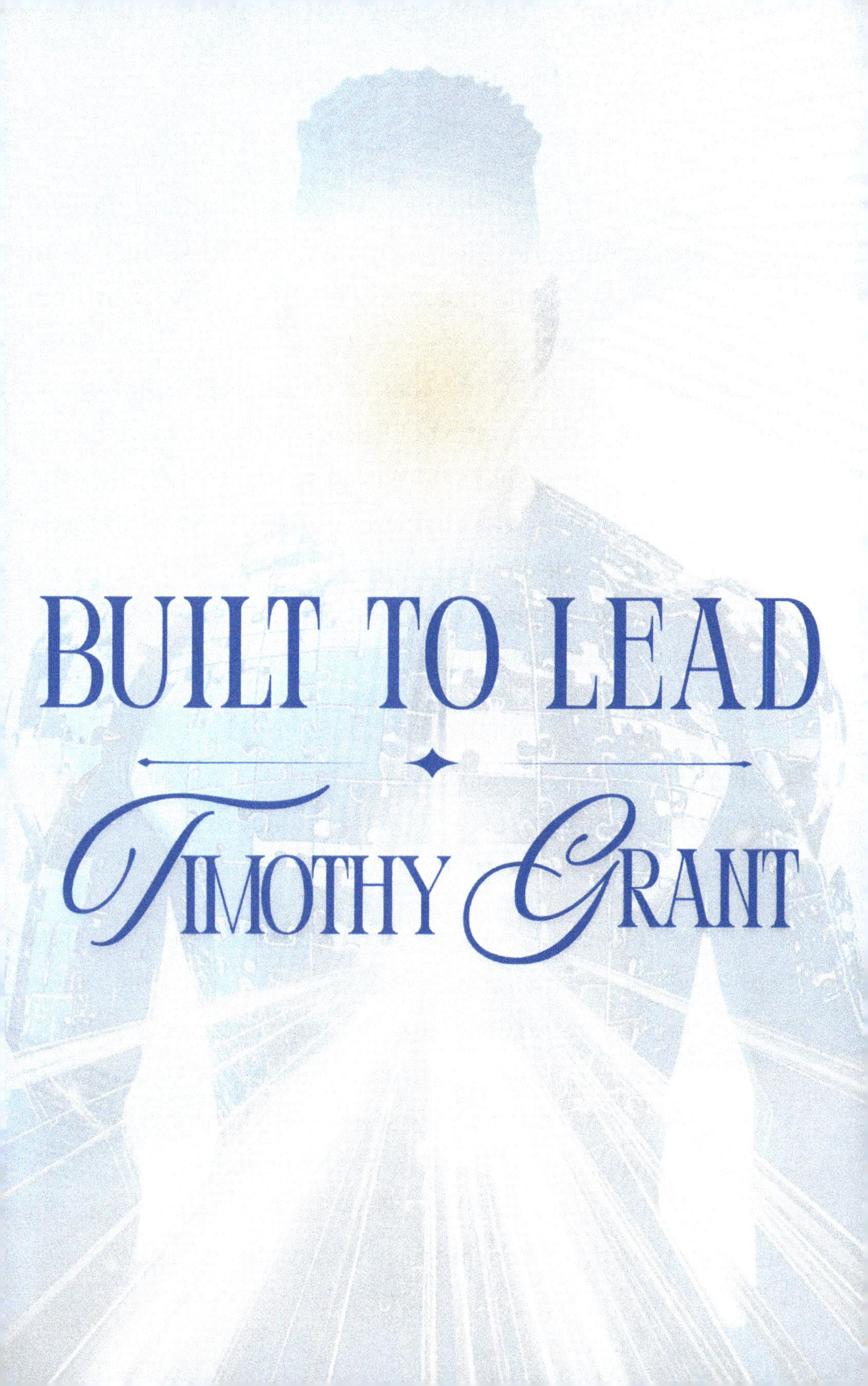
BUILT TO LEAD
TIMOTHY GRANT

Built by His Design

Leadership is not a human invention; it is God's design. From the beginning, He called men not just to exist, but to lead with vision, strength, boldness and humility. Scripture reminds us that we were created to rule (**Genesis 1:26-28**), steward (**Genesis 2:15**), and walk in dominion (**Psalm 8:4-6**). Leadership within the context of God's Kingdom is defined not by titles but by the responsibilities entrusted to individuals. It involves exemplifying the character of Christ and confidently fulfilling one's designated role. Though it may seem counterintuitive in today's culture, Kingdom leadership guides others toward *following* Christ.

My earliest glimpse of Kingdom Leadership came through my father, Bishop Easton Grant. He modeled what it meant to lead by Christ's design. He did not demand respect; he lived in a way that earned it.

His consistent embodiment of humility, compassion, selflessness and faith left an imprint on me. I remember seeing him in various difficult situations and yet he was calm in conflict, gracious in correction, and consistent in devotion. He wasn't just a church leader; he was a Kingdom man, a leader at home, loved by the community. Although he was highly esteemed, watching him showed me that leadership was not just about his title or position but about presence.

That was my defining moment: realizing that leadership is first about who you are, before it is about what you do and who you lead. His example made it undeniable that effective leadership makes a difference. Being a Kingdom man is a charge that we must boldly accept and walk in it. Not everyone has had the opportunity to see this kind of kingdom leadership firsthand, but the principles that I saw in my father are laid out in the pages of Scripture for all to see. It is plain that leadership is a mantle to carry, not just a title to hold.

The call is clear: men are charged to lead boldly (*1 Kings 2:2-3*), reflecting the character of Christ in every aspect of life; this is what I refer to as counter-culture leadership.

Counter-culture Leadership

In today's world, it's easy to notice that popular culture often puts a spotlight on people who have power, fame, or a big following—even if their character doesn't match up. Maybe you've worked with, or seen, leaders who seem impressive on the outside, but behind the scenes, they don't live out the values they talk about, oftentimes acting in ways that are the complete opposite of what they espouse. In today's society, it can sometimes seem like it's more important to have a big name or a large social media presence than it is to care for others or do the right thing. This reminds me of how Jesus called out the Pharisees—they looked perfect on the surface, but their hearts weren't in the right place (Matthew 23:27).

But Kingdom leadership calls us to something deeper. It's not about building your own brand or making yourself look good—it's about pointing people to God and making a real difference in their lives. I've seen a variety of leaders in my own life—some who got results, but not all of them led with godly character. In fact, a lot of what "works" in the business world or in society comes straight from the Bible, even if people don't realize it. For example, the book of Proverbs emphasizes the importance of having a vision, this is a common leadership approach. But vision in and of itself will not guarantee success.

Being successful by the world's standards isn't the same as being a Kingdom leader. One can be effective, even admired, and still miss the mark of what God calls us to be.

To be a Kingdom leader today means standing out from the crowd—choosing a different path, with different motives and values. It means leading in a way that might not always get you applause or recognition, but it reflects the heart and character of Jesus. That's what it means to walk boldly in the mantle of Kingdom leadership: being willing to go against the grain for something greater than yourself, and to lead with humility, integrity, and a focus on God's Kingdom instead of your own. This is counter-culture leadership at its core.

Think about leaders you have come across. This could be a boss at work, a coach, or even someone in your community. You might notice a leader who's more interested in being admired or staying in control than actually helping their team. They might avoid tough feedback, want to make all the decisions themselves, or seem obsessed with getting noticed. That kind of leadership can leave people feeling unheard and disconnected. The Bible actually warns us about this: leaders who manipulate, avoid accountability, and chase recognition. These leaders aren't following God's example, but they're still considered leaders, nonetheless.

Kingdom leaders, however, are open to feedback, seek out accountability, and stay humble. It's the difference between someone who's proud and ends up isolated, and someone who's humble and ends up respected (see **Proverbs 18:12**).

Now, consider "counter-culture leadership"—maybe you know someone at work who always questions "the way things have always been done." This person isn't afraid to try new ideas, challenge old habits, or push for changes that make things better. They inspire others to think creatively and not just accept the status quo. When it's done with the right heart—grounded in kindness and integrity—counter-culture leadership can bring out the best in a team. But if it's just about being different for the sake of it, or if there's no clear set of values, it can confuse people or even divide them. The key is making sure that bold leadership is always rooted in positive, constructive values, so that everyone feels supported and knows what the group stands for.

As the name suggests, counter-culture leadership will come across as challenging, to most, initially. God calls you to be courageous to accomplish the task that He has given you. You may recall great leaders in the Bible whose leadership seemed to divide, but ultimately brought forth great change. Moses, as he led God's people from Egypt, was a counter-culture leader. Joshua, the great military leader, employed unorthodox methods to gain victory as a counter-culture leader. Gideon who took, what appeared to be, a severely undermanned army to war, was a counter-culture leader. Jesus, who consistently challenged the status quo of the day, was a Kingdom centered, counter-culture leader. God is challenging your character. He's looking for those who are willing to go against the trends of this world to lead in a way that honors Him.

Character to Lead

To further grasp what Kingdom leadership looks like, let us reflect on the case studies of men who carried the mantle with courage and humility. These stories are not just ancient history; they provide practical blueprints for us today.

Looking closer at the lives of other biblical figures in Jesus, Paul, Abraham, and Peter, we see that their stories aren't just ancient tales, they offer real lessons for us right now.

Jesus didn't lead by seeking the spotlight or holding the highest position; instead, He humbled Himself, washing the feet of His followers and caring for those who were often overlooked. He was an excellent example of one who holds dominion, yet His humility kept him focused on the Father's mission.

Paul's journey teaches us resilience; he faced prison, misunderstanding, slander, shipwrecks, and persecution, yet he never stopped encouraging others or planting seeds of hope. Resilience is a key characteristic for a Kingdom Leadership.

Abraham's faith stands out; even when he didn't know exactly where God was leading him, he trusted enough to step forward and bring his family along. Abraham believed in God's instructions which empowered him to follow through.

Peter's life shows us that mistakes don't disqualify us, he went from denying Jesus to boldly leading after Pentecost, proving that failure can be a fresh start rather than the end. Kingdom Leaders will make mistakes, sometimes major mistakes, but learning from these setbacks can have tremendous impact.

What's remarkable is that, with the exception of Jesus, none of these leaders were perfect. They had flaws, struggles, and messy pasts, but God still used them in incredible ways. Their lives remind us that true leadership isn't about having it all together but being willing to serve, to trust when the way isn't clear, to keep going through hardships, and to let God redeem our failures. These examples make it clear: you don't have to be flawless to make a difference, you just have to be open, humble, and willing to let God work through your story. Even with glaring flaws, you can boldly take the mantle of Kingdom Leadership. Here are even more examples of flawed men who took up the mantle.

Moses was reluctant at first, questioning his speech and ability, yet God chose him to lead Israel out of bondage. His journey shows us that leadership is not about natural talent but about obedience to God's call. Despite opposition and personal shortcomings, Moses remained faithful, interceding for the people and leading them toward promise. This journey was not without opposition from both those he led, and those who opposed him. But Moses persevered. This teaches us that the leader God calls, He equips.

Nehemiah is another striking example. As a cupbearer, he had no royal authority, yet his burden for Jerusalem propelled him into leadership. Through prayer, planning, and perseverance, he rebuilt the walls in record time. His leadership was marked by vision and resilience—he worked with one hand on the task and the other ready to defend against opposition (*Nehemiah 4:17*). Leaders today must embrace Nehemiah's balance of spiritual discernment and practical strategy.

David, the shepherd boy turned king, shows us that leadership is often tested in obscurity before it is displayed publicly. He learned to fight lions and bears before he ever faced the giant, Goliath. Leaders must embrace the hidden seasons of preparation, trusting that God uses the unseen battles to prepare us for visible ones. David's psalms also remind us that leaders must stay connected to worship and intimacy with God.

Success, unfortunately, has been known to lead people astray. Consider how many great men of God we've seen fall due to massive "success" or blessings from God. Many Kingdom Leaders begin by adhering to the Kingdom traits exhibited by God's chosen, but success can sometimes breed toxic leadership traits if one is not careful. Success, while becoming distant from God, can lead to toxic traits that threaten Kingdom Leadership.

Kingdom Traits vs. Toxic Leadership Traits

Kingdom Traits	Toxic Traits
Humility (Philippians 2:3-5)	Pride
Servanthood (Mark 10:45)	Manipulation
Authenticity (2 Corinthians 1:12)	Hypocrisy
Accountability (Ecclesiastes 4:9-10)	Isolation

The qualifications for Kingdom leadership go beyond worldly measures. They require humility, servanthood, authenticity, and accountability. Biblical models teach that leadership is not about control, show of strength, or outward success. Kingdom Leadership is serving others, leading with love, and nurturing those entrusted to one's care. The Kingdom leader protects, equips, and presses toward growth, continually refining his heart and motives to align with God's standards.

Peter admonishes leaders; *To the elders among you, I appeal as a fellow elder and a witness of Christ's sufferings who also will share in the glory to be revealed: Be shepherds of*

*God's flock that is under your care, watching over them—not because you must, but because you are willing, as God wants you to be; not pursuing dishonest gain, but eager to serve; not lording it over those entrusted to you, but being examples to the flock. **1 Peter 5:1-3***

Kingdom leadership isn't about bossing people around—it's about leading in a way that honors God. Instead of chasing power or control, Kingdom leaders serve others while setting an example worth following. Here's what a practical Kingdom leader looks like:

- **Protector:** A good leader protects the people they're responsible for. Just like Abraham prayed to save the lives of the righteous prior to the destruction of the city of Sodom, leaders care enough to step in and help when others are in trouble. Jesus said, "I am the good shepherd. The good shepherd lays down his life for the sheep" (*John 10:11*).

- **Lead by Example**: Leaders aren't just telling others what to do, they're showing it with their own lives. Paul said, "Follow me as I follow Christ" (*1 Corinthians 11:1*). And in *1 Timothy 4:12*, we're told to set an example in the way we talk, act, love, believe, and live with purity.

- **Lead with Love**: Leadership without love doesn't mean much. Jesus showed love by washing His disciples' feet, teaching us that real leaders serve others. As *1 Corinthians 13:2* reminds us, if we don't have love, our leadership is empty.

- **Nurturer**: Leaders help others grow. Peter went from making mistakes to helping build up and encourage others. *Ephesians 4:11-12* says leaders equip people so everyone can serve and make a difference.

- **Committed to Growth**: Good leaders never stop learning or improving. Paul kept pushing forward, and *Proverbs 27:17* says, *"Iron sharpens iron, so one man sharpens another."* Leaders help each other get better.

Kingdom leadership, at its core, is about showing up for others; serving, loving, protecting, and helping others become who they're meant to be. Is it always easy? Definitely not. But when we lead this way, we honor God, and it's totally worth it. The more we lean into these qualities, the bolder we'll walk for Christ.

I'm always telling the guys around me that Kingdom leadership isn't just something you do at church on Sunday morning. It's way bigger than that. Our leadership should show in how we love our wives (and those around us), how we raise our kids (and interact with others), how we go about our jobs (and the effort we put in to any task that's given to us), how we handle friendships (and acquaintances), how we get involved in our neighborhoods (and the broader world around us), or how we serve without needing an elevated title.

Too often, we shrink Kingdom leadership down to what happens inside the church walls, but God's call is for every area of our lives. Living out this kind of leadership is our mandate, and we can only get there when our character matches the calling. Let us be men who walk worthy of the call God's put on us at any cost!

Cost to Lead

Here's one thing I know for sure: if you've been given much, much is expected of you. People often think leadership looks glamorous, but the truth is, Kingdom Leadership costs you a tremendous amount. To lead well, you've got to toss out the phony ideas about what leadership really is. People say leadership is all about power, prestige and being in control. But real leadership is about serving (*Mark 10:43-45*). Some say leaders can never show weakness. The real story? God's power actually shines brightest when we admit we're weak (*2 Corinthians 12:9*). And while the world measures leaders by their success, God measures us by our faithfulness (*Matthew 25:21*).

Taking up the mantle of leadership isn't easy. It's tough, and it comes with a cost. Be prepared to pour out your time and energy; sometimes you will even have to put your reputation on the line. In **Matthew 16:13,** Jesus asked the disciples, *"Who do men say that I am?"* This is a question of reputation. Some may perceive you differently from reality, or even the way you see yourself. This can create conflict. As a result, you must prepare for opposition.

People will likely talk behind your back while appearing to be supportive to your face. Jesus faced this with one of his disciples, Judas Iscariot, who ultimately betrayed him to the Roman authorities. During their last encounter, Judas greeted Jesus with a kiss (**Mark 14:44-45**). There will likely be long stretches when you're grinding away with no recognition.

The truth is, Kingdom leaders stick it out through hard times. They actively refuse to exhibit toxic leadership traits. Kingdom leaders also resist manipulation and keep showing up even when things get messy. Kingdom Leadership is seldom glamorous.

I'll be honest, the cost of Kingdom leadership is high. You'll sacrifice sleep, comfort, and sometimes relationships. Jesus didn't sugarcoat it; He said, *"Whoever wants to be my disciple must deny themselves and take up their cross daily and follow me"* (**Luke 9:23**). That means every day you carry the weight, responsibility, criticism, and the discipline of doing what's right, even when it's hard.

But here's the thing: the cost doesn't even come close to the reward of hearing, "Well done, good and faithful servant." As Kingdom leaders, we have to say "no" to what we feel like doing, "no" to letting our flesh call the shots, and "no" to taking revenge, even when everything in us wants to. Sometimes leading means loving and serving people who barely notice or acknowledge your sacrifice, or worse, actively shun your efforts. I've watched great leaders go the extra mile for folks who don't appreciate them, simply because they've learned to "deny themselves" and keep leading like Kingdom men.

Honestly, the reward isn't here on earth. Kingdom leadership will sometimes leave you feeling used, overlooked, and even hurt, but God's approval significantly outweighs anybody else's applause. The cost might be friendships, finances, and/or your comfort. It will definitely cost your pride. But it's all about building the Kingdom. The price is high, but the eternal reward—the chance to hear "Well done, good and faithful servant"- makes it all worth it.

Cultivating Leaders (Legacy)

A huge part of Kingdom leadership is raising up new leaders—leaving a legacy that outlives us. This wasn't just

Jesus' priority with His disciples; we see it all through Scripture—Paul pouring into Timothy, Elijah mentoring Elisha, Moses preparing Joshua. My own dad modeled it for me, and I've watched countless other Kingdom men live it out, too. When you step into Kingdom leadership, you quickly realize: this is way bigger than you. The vision isn't supposed to end with us—God's story moves forward through every generation.

Young men, let me talk straight to you: the mantle of leadership isn't just for "someday"—it's on you now. The world desperately needs men who are bold enough to stand for Christ, even when it's not popular. Don't wait until you feel "qualified." Abraham followed God without a roadmap. Don't let your mistakes hold you back—Peter went from denying Jesus to preaching with power. Don't let fear of criticism stop you—Paul kept running his race despite all kinds of opposition. Leading takes guts, but remember: it's not about your strength. God gave Gideon everything he needed, and He'll do the same for you.

You might say to yourself, well those are great MEN, well there are several examples of young men, in the Bible, who also exhibited great Kingdom Leadership as well including a young David, who I mentioned earlier and even Joseph who showed great Kingdom Leadership while in prison. But one of my favorites is the prophet Daniel and his three buddies,

Shadrach, Meshach, and Abednego, during their time in the foreign land of Babylon. Daniel lived in a manner that reflected the Kingdom Leadership traits mentioned previously, and as a result, Daniel and his friends honored God in a way that influenced the king, and they were elevated to positions of influence due to their authenticity, faithfulness, and accountability to God.

Here's my challenge: Develop discipline, stay humble, and chase after God every day. Reject the world's twisted ideas about leadership—power trips, ego, using people—and instead, copy Jesus' servant heart. Lead like this, and you'll change families, churches, and even whole communities.

Kingdom leadership is all about advancing Christ's Kingdom and making an impact that lasts. Our call is to surrender daily, serve with integrity, and always point others to Jesus—not ourselves. The mantle has to pass on. So, encourage the next guy, walk boldly, don't get distracted by fake versions of leadership, and keep humility and discipline front and center. Stay focused on what matters for eternity, because nothing you do for the Lord ever gets wasted. At the end of the day, what counts isn't applause or attention—it's God's approval and the impact you make on lives for generations.

So, to the young men stepping up: walk boldly in your calling. This world will tempt you with all kinds of counterfeits—power without real purpose, influence without integrity, charisma without character. Don't buy it. "Be strong and courageous… for the Lord your God will be with you wherever you go." Lead with love. Protect the people God puts in your path. Stay teachable. And live so that when people look at you, they see Christ.

Seasoned men, you understand well that life, leadership, and love each carry their share of challenges. Yet as long as God grants you breath, your role in advancing Kingdom leadership remains vital. The call to lead and to leave a godly impact does not come with an expiration date. It is not sufficient to simply lament the direction of this generation; it is essential that you rise, embrace the authority entrusted to you, and walk boldly in the mantle of Kingdom leadership. YOU are needed. YOU are valued. And YOU have been uniquely designed and positioned for such a time as this.

Conclusion

Living by God's design means giving up control daily and letting Him lead.

As you are led by Christ, each day, you'll face the challenge of choice: leading as the world leads or leading in a countercultural way. For this, you'll need the courage to "choose life."

Every day you must consider your character. This means reflecting on the day's decisions, asking yourself if your character aligned with that of a Kingdom leader. For this you'll need wisdom.

At the conclusion of each day, it's wise to reflect on the cost of Kingdom Leadership and ask God for your daily needs as you lead for His glory.

And every day, you'll want to challenge yourself to cultivate Kingdom leaders to carry the mantle in your absence. For this, you'll need humility to understand it's not about you.

These daily reminders are essential. Preparing to surrender fully to Kingdom Leadership is a challenging task that can only be reached by connectedness with God. For me to do this successfully, I:

- Start each day with prayer and reading the Bible,

- Remain transparent and honest with a few close friends who help keep me on track,

- Love my family well,

- Help my church and community in real, tangible ways,

- Check my heart, asking, "Am I making this about me, or am I helping others see Jesus?" Am I serving for recognition or for God's glory?

A long-term perspective can guide Kingdom Leadership. The goal is not to build personal empires, but to work toward a mission that endures beyond immediate recognition. While public acknowledgment may fade, the influence Kingdom leaders create will certainly have everlasting effects. Kingdom Leaders who persist with purpose understand that their actions contribute to something greater than themselves.

Kingdom Leadership is about positively shaping others' lives. Following examples set by notable historical figures, Kingdom leaders can leave behind legacies rather than just memories. It is beneficial to reflect on how one's leadership can serve the well-being of future generations, encouraging qualities such as courage, integrity, and compassion.

Consider these questions to evaluate how you can strengthen your approach to purposeful leadership so that you, too can walk boldly in the mantle of Kingdom Leadership:

- Recall when you first felt called to lead. Was it at school, home, or elsewhere?

- What misconceptions about leadership have you realized are untrue?

- Which biblical leader's journey resonates with you most, and why?

- Do you notice habits that might negatively affect those you lead, and how could you change them?

- In your daily interactions, how do you support and encourage those who rely on you?

Then begin to come up with practical steps on how to take up the mantle and run with it. While traits and stories inspire us, leaders need practical guidance. Here are practices that strengthen a leader's walk:

- Start and end each day with prayer and reflection for clarity.

- Build a support network of mentors (who have further experience in Kingdom leadership), accountability partners (who walk beside you along your journey), and others (whose journey you support to enhance their Kingdom leadership).

- Monitor the details in several areas of your life, including—but not limited to—your time, your health, your finances, and your character.

- Serve without seeking recognition.

- Regularly assess your motives for leadership.

Living by God's design means surrendering every day, no shortcuts, no exceptions.

Surrender is a simple concept but it's not always easy. I have to start my day with prayer and getting into Scripture, or I'm all over the place. I lean on a couple of trusted brothers to keep me honest and accountable, because it's way too easy to drift. I try my best to love my family with consistency, not just when I feel like it, and I make it a point to serve my church and community with integrity, even when no one's watching.

But here's the real gut check: Am I pointing people to myself, or to Christ? Is my serving about being noticed, or is it actually for God's glory? These questions keep me grounded and remind me why I lead in the first place.

Kingdom Leadership ALWAYS points to the King. If it doesn't, then it's not Kingdom Leadership.

BROKEN BUT BUILT

BRIAN GAFFNEY

The Mask

For forty years, I wore a mask and built walls. I thought I was protecting myself, but I didn't realize I was building my own prison.

Brick by brick, defense by defense, I constructed an elaborate fortress around my heart. Every wall had a purpose. Every barrier had a reason. The wall of approval kept me performing. The Wall of protection kept me running. The Wall around my heart kept me from being hurt. The Wall of Self-Suppression kept me small and safe. The Wall of Codependency kept me from ever being alone with myself or with God.

From the outside, I looked successful and talented. People saw confidence and charisma, gifts and capability. What they didn't see was the man suffocating inside his own fortress, exhausting himself maintaining a façade, dying slowly behind walls that promised safety but delivered isolation.

The mindset I built to protect my emotions ultimately became the walls that enslaved me.

I was never alone, yet I was completely lonely. People surrounded me, yet nobody truly knew me. I had built a prison so secure that even I couldn't find my way out. "Whoever isolated himself seeks his own desire; He rages against all wise judgment." (Proverbs 18:1 I thought I was wise... I was a fool.

This is how those walls came down—not by my strength, but by my breaking. This is how God entered through the wound I desperately tried to avoid. This is how a man imprisoned by his own defenses finally became free.

The First Crack: When Excellent Became Dangerous

I grew up in a middle-class home in Bed Stuy, Brooklyn, with both parents and four older siblings. As the youngest of five, I learned to navigate life in the slipstream of those who came before me. Responsibilities landed on me last, and I took full advantage of that positioning—not realizing I was training myself in avoidance, teaching myself that the path of least resistance was the safest path to walk.

In our house, emotions weren't discussed. You could cry if you broke your arm or faced some catastrophic event, but telling someone how you actually felt? That language didn't exist in our home. My job was simple: be well-behaved and perform well in school. For the most part, I did exactly that. I stayed small. I played it safe. I colored inside the lines.

Then one summer changed everything.

I went down south at five-foot-eight and came back at six-foot-three. Five inches in a few months. But it wasn't just my height that transformed- I got better. Stronger. Faster. More capable. And in our neighborhood, that meant everything, because basketball wasn't just a game- it was currency. Being nice on the court could grant you safety, popularity, and protection. It was a rite of passage, and suddenly, I had the physical tools to dominate!

My older Brother Eric was my role model. He was one of the top players in our neighborhood. I looked up to him, studied his game, and wanted to be just like him.

But when I returned from that summer transformed, I became something I never intended to be a threat.

There was one moment that changed the trajectory of my entire life.

We were playing basketball one summer evening in a crowded park.

I saw a quick opening, and my eyes lit up. I quickly gathered all my power and strength and went up for a thunderous dunk—confident, unguarded, fully myself for maybe the first time. Then, Mid—air, Eric snatched me down so violently that he ripped my t-shirt completely off my body. The sound of that thick jersey fabric ripping. The crushing pain in my hip from falling onto the concrete. I felt humiliated in front of everybody watching.

But more than the physical pain, the message that moment burned into my soul was that being your best is dangerous.

I can still feel the realization settling over me like a death sentence. If my own brother—my hero, the person I admired most—would react with such aggression to my excellence, what would everyone else do? If I could surpass Eric, one of the top players around, I could potentially be better than most. But greatness, I learned that day, came with a cost. Outshining others meant inviting jealousy, envy, retaliation, and isolation.

So, I made a decision that would haunt me for decades.

I decided to shrink, to scale back, to be less than who God created me to be. I told myself a lie and believed it with every fiber of my being: Be less and keep the peace at all times. "Your safety is found in smallness."

That day on the basketball court, the first wall went up. I chose who I thought I needed to be over who God created me to be. I began the exhausting work of managing everyone else's comfort at the expense of my own soul.

*"There is a way that seems right to a man, but its end is the way to death." (**Proverbs 14:12**).*

I thought I had found wisdom and safety. What I actually found was bondage.

The Walls That Imprisoned Me

Once the first wall went up, the rest followed like a blueprint for self-destruction. Each one seemed necessary at the time, each one promised protection, and each one delivered a different kind of death.

The Wall Of Approval

I needed others to validate me. Every decision, every move, every version of myself was calculated to earn someone's approval. I created an outward dependency on everyone except my Creator. Performance became my identity. If I could just be good enough, talented enough, maybe I'd finally feel secure.

Strange as it may seem, basketball became my shield. As long as I was playing at the height of my athleticism, no one could see that I was hurting on the inside. The court was where I could control the narrative, manage the perception, and get the validation I craved. Even then, God was trying to get in, whispering truth through the noise, but my ego wouldn't let

Him. I had built my own salvation through achievement, and I didn't need saving.

The Wall Of Protection

I trained myself to flee when facing harsh treatment, envy, jealousy, which the total opposite for competing in any arena. The basketball taught me that excellence invited aggression, so I developed a mindset of escape. Run before you get hurt. Leave before they can reject you. Disappear before the conflict escalates.

I chose safety instead of surrender, containment instead of commitment. I became passive instead of passionate. Every potential confrontation was a threat to be avoided, every difficult conversation a danger to be sidestepped. At 14, I convinced myself this was wisdom, maturity, and self-control. No, it was cowardice dressed in respectable clothes.

The Wall Around My Heart

I built a fortress around my capacity to love. "Never give your heart to a woman," I heard growing up, and I followed that rule. I wouldn't let any woman truly in, wouldn't commit to anything serious or anyone—not because I didn't want to, but because the mask I wore wouldn't allow it. The real me was too dangerous to expose, too vulnerable to risk, and too broken to offer.

So, I kept relationships surface-level, with one foot always outside the door and my heart always half-engaged. People surrounded me, but I was utterly alone. I had friends but no intimacy. I had relationships, but no real connection. The wall around my heart kept me safe from rejection, but it also kept me safe from love, from knowing and being known, the thing my soul was starving for.

The Wall Of-Self Suppression

I deliberately retarded my gifts. On the basketball court and every other arena of life, I played beneath my capabilities. I made myself a smaller target, dimmed my light, and held back what God had given me. The exhaustion of constantly suppressing who you really are is a special kind of torture— like trying to hold a beach ball under water for 40 years.

Every major opportunity became a threat. Every moment that called for my full self, became a moment to shrink back. I told myself I was being humble, considerate, and a team player. I was being a coward. I was burying the talents God gave me because I was afraid of what would happen if I actually used them.

The Wall Of Codependency

I never did anything alone. Ever. I always had family around, friends nearby, or a girlfriend attached. I used people as a buffer between me and my own soul. Between me and where the silence of God was waiting. I never knew who I was by myself, and I made sure I was never by myself.

This wasn't community, this wasn't fellowship, this was avoidance. I was using relationships to run from relationships—with myself, with God, and with the truth. I had become so dependent on the presence of others that I lost all sense of who I was in their absence.

The Prison Revealed

Here's what I didn't understand for forty years: these walls all created dependency on myself instead of God. I made myself the protector, the advisor, the deliverer, the shield. I had taken on roles that were never mine to carry. I had replaced God with my own self-made defenses, my own strategies for survival, my own plans for safety.

But God is the protector. God is the advisor. God is the deliverer and the shield. Not me. Never me.

The walls that promised safety delivered slavery. The defenses that promised protection delivered isolation. The fortress I built to keep pain out kept life out, love out, and God out.

"Unless the Lord builds the house, those who build it labor in vain." (Psalm 127:1)

I had labored for forty years building a house that was really a tomb. And I was dying inside it one day at a time, one wall at a time, one lie at a time.

God Knocking At The Walls

God chased me even when I was running. Every failure was an invitation to surrender. And every loss was him trying to get my attention. But I became an expert at ignoring the knock at the door.

The first major blow came through a devastating real estate deal. Two hundred thousand dollars lost. The kind of financial hit that sets a family back years, that shakes your confidence in your own judgment, that forces you to question everything. God was speaking to me then—loud and clear. But only partially listened. I took just enough of the lesson to survive, patched up the wound, reinforced the walls, and kept moving. I was convinced that I could rebuild what was lost through my own strength, my own hustle, my own determination.

Then there was a pattern I couldn't ignore: I was a notorious non-finisher. I'd start strong, begin with passion and vision, and then fade before crossing the finish line. Projects left incomplete. Goals abandoned halfway. Relationships that never got to depth. It was a wake-up call, another alarm blaring in my soul. But instead of stopping to listen I just turned up the volume on my excuses.

God was persistent—relentless. Every setback was his megaphone. Every failure was His mercy trying to arrest my descent. He blocked my path, put obstacles in my way, and did everything to get me to stop running and start surrendering.

"Therefore, I will block her path with thorn bushes; I will wall her in so that she cannot find her way" (**Hosea 2:6**)

But I had spent decades perfecting the Art of self-protection. I knew how to rebuild walls faster than they could crumble, patch cracks, reinforce defenses, and convince myself that one attempt at self-sacrifice would finally work.

It wouldn't. And God knew what I didn't: sometimes the only way to save a man is to let everything fall apart.

The Breaking: Rock Bottom

I can't name names. I can only name the brokenness. The shattering of the one wall I thought could never be breached. It was the blow I didn't see coming, delivered by someone I would have never expected, cutting deeper than any pain I'd ever known.

And it dropped me to my knees.

All the walls came tumbling down at once. The Wall of Approval crumbled—No amount of performance could fix this. The Wall of Protection collapsed—there was nowhere left to run. The wall around my heart exploded—The pain had found its way in despite everything. The Wall of Self Suppression disintegrated —I had nothing left to hide, no energy to hold back. The Wall of Codependency fell—everyone was gone, and it was just me, broken, alone, with nowhere left to turn.

(Psalm 119:71) *"It is good for me that I have been afflicted, that I might learn thy statutes."*

The mask that I had worn for forty years finally cracked beyond repair

For the first time in my life, I had no defense. No strategy. No plan. No way to manage the narrative or control the outcome. I was completely exposed, utterly helpless, absolutely shattered. And in that moment of total devastation, I discovered something that changed everything...

"God enters through the wound..."- Carl Jung

It was the wound of betrayal that cracked me open. When my defenses were shattered, when my pride was silenced, when my own strength failed—something greater entered. Someone greater. The God I had been running from, the God I had been replacing with my own self-made salvation, the God who had been knocking on my walls for forty years, finally had access to the broken man inside.

"The Lord is close to the brokenhearted and saves those who are crushed in spirit." (Psalm 34:18)

I was brokenhearted. I was crushed in spirit. And for the first time in my life, I was close to God—not because I had finally got strong enough to reach Him, but because I had finally got weak enough to let him reach me.

The betrayal wasn't my end; it was my beginning. What was meant to break and destroy me, God used to build and restore me. The wound that could have left me devastated became the opening through which His light flooded in. The breaking that felt like death became the birth of something I had never known: true surrender.

"The sacrifices of God are a broken spirit; and a contrite heart, O God, you will not despise." (Psalm 51:17)

I had been broken enough to totally surrender. And finally, on my knees, I rose not as the same man who had fallen, but as one fortified by fire, rebuilt with purpose, and anchored in unshakable faith.

Rebuilt: From Broken To Built

Total surrender changes everything.

When I finally let God be God—My Protector, My advisor, My deliverer, My shield—He began rebuilding what forty years of self-reliance and spiritual strongholds had destroyed. Not with my strength, but with His. *"My grace is sufficient is for you, for my power is made perfect in weakness"* **(2 Corinthians 12:9)**

The rebuilding hasn't been easy. Learning to live without the mask after forty years is terrifying and liberating in equal measure. Some days I still feel the ghost of those walls, the instinct to shrink back, to protect, to perform. But I'm learning to live in the freedom Christ purchased for me, to stand in the identity He gives rather than the one I manufacture.

"Therefore, if anyone is in Christ, the new creation has come: the old has gone, the new is here," **(2 Corinthians 5:17)**. I am being rebuilt. Not Perfect. But authentic. Not performing, but present. Not hiding, but healing. The man God always intended is finally emerging from the rubble of the fortress I built.

And now I'm writing this chapter for you—the man reading this while wearing your own mask, suffocating behind your own walls. Maybe you've told yourself the same lies I did:

that your walls keep you safe, that your mask keep you acceptable, that you can manage on your own.

Brother, hear me: The walls that promise protection, deliver prison. You cannot heal what you will not reveal. The mask is killing you slowly, and the fortress you've built is really a tomb.

Men, hear me—if it takes breaking you to build you, then let God break you. Stop clinging to the masks, stop running from the call, and fall on your knees in full surrender. Because the man you're meant to be is only forged through the fire, pressure, and the weight of his will. Be relentless, be desperate, be unyielding in your pursuit of Him—even if it crushes you—because it is far better to be broken in God's hands than to stand whole in your own. That's not weakness—the strength of a man rebuilt, fortified, and unstoppable!

Just as Job declared, *"But He knows how I take when he has tested me, I will come forth as gold. (**Job 23:10**)*

Scripture And Quotes

2 Corinthians 12:9 (Power in Weakness)

Psalm 34:18 (Close to the brokenhearted)

Psalm 51:17 (New Creation)

Matthew 7:24-27 (Build on the Rock)

Job 23:10 (God is our Redeemer)

Proverbs 14:12 (Way that seems right)

2 Corinthians 1:3-4 (Comfort to comfort others)

2 Corinthians 5:17 (New Creature in Christ)

Psalm 119:71 (Good Affliction)

Hosea 2:6 (Blocked Paths)

Psalm 127:1 (Except The Lord build the house)

Proverbs 18:1 (Separated for wisdom)

About the Storytellers

BISHOP Rufus Mahon

Born to the late Rufus Glen Mahon, Sr. and Mildred Mahon in 1963, Bishop Rufus Glen Mahon, Jr. was a child full of ambition and great vision. As the fifth child, he embodies the grace of God in every part of his life. After surviving a near-death heart attack that doctors could only describe as an anomaly, Bishop Mahon accepted Jesus Christ as his personal Savior in 1989.

In May 2009, Bishop Mahon married the love of his life, Pastor Allison Mahon. From their union, one child was born, Josiah Mahon. Together, they have five children and enjoy serving in their family ministry.

Bishop Rufus Mahon currently leads Preserving Life Center in Harlem, NY, alongside his wife, Pastor Allison Mahon. In 2020, he established By His Design Men's Ministry, which has guided men into manhood, and this book project is a direct result of that work.

Bishop Rufus Mahon received an Honorary Doctorate Degree in 2023, a Pastoral Counseling Certification from the National Association of Christian Counselors in 2025, and numerous awards and certifications of service.

Bishop Rufus Mahon desires to see God's people grow and reach all God has planned for them, especially men. Through the efforts of By His Design Men's Ministry, he is working toward that goal, one man at a time.

BRIAN BENTLEY

Brian Bentley was born in Macon, Georgia, on July 14, 1977. He is the oldest of two children born to Ronda Bentley. Brian lived with his mother until age 12, when he moved in with his grandmother. He remained with his grandmother until he turned 18, a pivotal age marked by a major life-changing event. His grandmother passed away following a freak medical accident during a routine hospital procedure. This loss led Brian to become cold and uncaring, resulting in poor choices and a tendency to run the streets. At age 20, he welcomed his first son, Tazman Williams, and has since been working to build a bond with him, despite years of incarceration.

Brian's first encounter with the prison system was at 21, and he spent ten years behind bars. After re-entering society, he was re-incarcerated in 2015 for another seven years, which he describes as his last encounter with the system. He was released in January 2021. Later that year, Brian married Min Charisse Bentley, the woman who supported him through his struggles. The couple has a son born in 2023, bringing them great joy. Through his marriage, Brian also gained two stepchildren, Cheyanne and Keith Crowder. He works full-time as a sanitation driver, but his ultimate dream is to become a filmmaker.

Earl Carpenter, Jr.

Earl was born and raised in Washington D.C. He is a loving husband and father to one girl, two boys, and seven grandchildren. He is currently retired from the federal government after working for twenty years as an Intelligence Officer. He is also an Army veteran who served for twenty years, mostly as a Spanish linguist.

Earl now attends Carmel Friendship Church (CFC) in Wesley Chapel, FL, under the leadership of Pastor Quincy Stratford. He is also a Deacon Emeritus at his home church, Trinidad Baptist Church, in District Heights, MD. Earl and his wife Charmaine, both retired, live a quiet life in Land O' Lakes, FL. They volunteer with several ministries at CFC, at the STRAZ Theater of the Arts in Tampa, FL, and for the Tampa Bay Buccaneers football team.

ERIC CARPENTER

Deacon Eric Carpenter is a man of God who understands and embraces God's blueprint for men. For more than 20 years, he has faithfully served under the leadership of Bishop Easton G. Grant, a true general in the Kingdom and his father-in-love, as Head Deacon and Traveling Armor Bearer at New Life Open Bible Church.

Alongside his wife, Pastor Sherill Grant-Carpenter, Deacon Eric leads the marriage ministry Forever Linked, where together they champion strong, God-centered marriages. The couple recently released their first book, a 31-Day Devotional for Married Couples entitled Forever Linked, designed to strengthen covenant relationships through prayer, reflection, and intentional connection.

Deacon Eric is also a family man. He and Pastor Sherill are the proud parents of five children and one granddaughter, and they are blessed with many spiritual sons and daughters whose lives they continue to pour into with wisdom and love.

His ministry extends beyond the church walls. He formerly served for seven years as the Men's Leader of Men of Valor at Deliverance Tabernacle Christian Center, where he equipped men to walk in godly integrity and strength. He also founded and led "Sunday Soul Food", a small group gathering that combined his gift for cooking with his heart for community—providing home-cooked Sunday meals and a welcoming table where individuals could share their struggles, victories, and faith journeys together.

Currently, Deacon Eric is also an active member of the By His Design Men's Group, under the leadership of Bishop Rufus Mahon, where he continues to grow alongside other men of faith in the pursuit of God's purpose and design for manhood.

Through his life, leadership, devotion to family, and love for God's people, Deacon Eric Carpenter is a living testimony of what it means to serve faithfully, lead humbly, and build others up according to the blueprint of God.

BISHOP PHILLIP CRICHLOW

Bishop M. Phillip Crichlow has been the pastor of the East Mount Olive Baptist Church in Harlem, NY, since 2003 and was consecrated as a bishop on January 30, 2010.

Before joining Gospel Cathedral Baptist Church, Bishop Crichlow was very active in gospel ministry. He was a member of Goodwill Baptist Church (1969), Ephesus SDA Church (1975-1989), and served as an assistant to Rev. Bernice A. King at Greater Rising Star Baptist Church (May 1995-February 1997), as well as at New Jerusalem COGIC.

As a member of Gospel Cathedral Baptist Church from 1989 to 1995, Bishop Crichlow was a dedicated musician playing drums for the 100 Voice Broadcasting Choir and served as a minister in the Outreach Ministry. He helped coordinate pickups for members, family, and guests, and organized church planting efforts.

Bishop also organized and/or pastored churches under the banner of Cathedral Baptist Church. New Life Cathedral Baptist Church and New Hope Cathedral Baptist Church were two of the churches where Bishop Crichlow evangelized, taught, and preached the Gospel of Jesus Christ.

He served as a Deacon and worked closely with Presiding Bishop James Eugene Berry on various boards, projects, and special services, including the Men's Department and Trustee Board.

His professional musical achievements are extensive and impressive. He's worked with the renowned "Ecstatistics" as their drummer for 47 years, the "Mighty Clouds of Joy" from April 1988 to December 1990, the "Soul Stirrers" and "Blind Boys of Alabama" from January 1991 to January 1995, and with "Shirley Caesar" and "James Cleveland" in 1989 and 1988, respectively.

Bishop Crichlow believes his latter shall be greater than his past and holds firm to his church's statement: "East Mount Olive Baptist Church: Where Everybody is Somebody!"

BRIAN GAFFNEY

After experiencing the transformative power of faith in Jesus Christ, Brian Gaffney is ready to pay it forward. As a survivor of childhood trauma and a champion of personal growth, Brian Gaffney has created a SaaS platform to equip others with essential financial life skills. Through his work and writing, he aims to restore hope and wholeness to those shaped by traumatic experiences who take the courageous step to heal. His contribution to The Men Of Valor is a testament to the redemptive power of faith and resilience through Christ Jesus.

REGINALD GANT

As a 5X author, trainer, and speaker, Reginald Gant is highly respected for many reasons. He is the Founder of Serve4Men, an organization dedicated to helping men improve themselves personally and professionally. The organization offers one-on-one coaching, group coaching, live events, meetups, and other programs aimed at men. Over the years, Reginald has confidently helped numerous working professionals find jobs and advance their careers.

Reginald Gant also has a wide range of talents. With more than 20 years of federal government experience, he has trained over 50,000 employees across federal agencies. As an entrepreneur for the past 12 years, Reginald currently helps small businesses, business owners, and entrepreneurs protect what matters most— themselves, their families, and their businesses. With the right resources, running a business can be smoother and more efficient. Reginald has successfully helped many small businesses access affordable legal advice and consultation to sustain and, more importantly, grow.

However, Reginald's greatest accomplishments are being happily married and being a father to five amazing children.
His life motto is simple: SERVE to be a blessing to others!

Timothy Grant

Pastor Timothy Grant is a passionate leader dedicated to worship, God's Word, and transforming lives through faith. He faithfully shares the unchanging truth of Scripture with power and conviction, delivering messages that touch hearts and motivate believers to deepen their relationship with the Lord. Through his ministry, many have come to know Christ personally and share stories of encouragement, healing, and renewal they have experienced. In addition to preaching, he also serves as a minstrel at New Life, using his musical talents to lead others into God's presence.

Beyond the pulpit, Timothy is a youth advocate, consultant, husband, and father, dedicated to faith, family, and community impact. With a heart for mentorship, he invests deeply in young people, guiding them to discover their purpose, build resilience, and lead with integrity. As a devoted husband and father of five, he exemplifies balance, commitment, and faith in action. Grounded in biblical values and driven by a vision for transformation, Timothy is committed to inspiring growth in others—whether in ministry, business, or everyday life.

Marvin Gross

Marvin Gross is a dedicated husband, father, son, and friend. A man of valor, his life reflects his deep love for God and His people. He is a passionate servant-leader who finds joy in helping others walk confidently in their God-given purpose. With a heart for ministry and a vision for transformation, Marvin pastors Reformation House of God, where he faithfully serves alongside his wife, equipping and empowering believers to live out their faith with courage and conviction.

Beyond the pulpit, Marvin is a community leader and mentor, committed to reaching young men from all backgrounds. His mission is to help them overcome societal pressures and statistics, breaking cycles that seek to limit their potential. He provides not only guidance but also hope, sharing wisdom to help them choose a better path and the strength to persevere against challenges.

Marvin is known widely as a man of wisdom, integrity, and great influence. His journey involves breaking barriers, overcoming obstacles, and consistently walking by faith. He continues to serve as a living example of resilience, vision, and unwavering trust in God's promises. A true visionary, Marvin inspires others to dream beyond limitations, pursue purpose with passion, and stay firm in the face of adversity.

Through his ministry, mentorship, and personal testimony, Marvin Gross has become a voice of encouragement and a beacon of faith—calling others higher, shaping lives, and leaving a lasting impact on both the church and the community.

ROYAL HUBBARD

Royal Hubbard is an MBE business owner, community leader, and dedicated mentor with over 25 years of experience in the maintenance industry. As the co-owner of The Royal Hub LLC, a catering company renowned for its flavorful dishes and community-focused service, Royal brings people together through food, culture, and compassion. In addition to his business pursuits, he works as a Property Manager, overseeing daily operations and ensuring quality living environments for residents across New York.

Beyond his professional endeavors, Royal is deeply involved in youth and community development. He proudly serves as the Cubmaster of Cub Scout Pack 627 in Rochdale Village, mentoring young boys in leadership, discipline, and respect for elders and God. As COO of the Family of Five Foundation, he helps organize impactful programs like community BBQs, Halloween events, sneaker giveaways, and family movie nights—initiatives aimed at fostering unity, responsibility, and joy among families.

In June 2024, Royal's unwavering dedication to service earned him the President's Volunteer Service Award (PVSA) for his outstanding community commitment. That same year, he was honored to serve on the Queens General Council under Queens Borough President Donovan Richards, contributing to local policy and community improvement efforts. He continues his involvement as a Queens General Council alumnus, staying active in civic and neighborhood development.

Among his many meaningful projects, the Father's Day BBQ stands out as one of Royal's proudest accomplishments. Started through the Family of Five Foundation, this event brings men together to celebrate fatherhood, brotherhood, and service—feeding the community with good food, great music, and genuine fellowship. Royal's lifelong mission is to empower youth, uplift families, and demonstrate that with faith, respect, and unity, every community can thrive.

REGINALD LANDRUM

Reginald B. Landrum is a relaxed yet powerful man of faith who walks in the gift of helps. Guided by the Holy Spirit, he uses his hands to fix what's broken and his words to uplift others. Known for his charisma and compassion, Reginald aims to reflect Christ in everything he does, restoring hope, rebuilding lives, and inspiring others to be their best in God's purpose.

"And thou shalt be called, The repairer of the breach, The restorer of paths to dwell." ~Isaiah 58:12

Emanuel Owens

Emanuel Owens was born to Hildagod Owens in 1966, as the oldest of three children. Emanuel spent most of his formative years with his late grandmother, Ruby Owens, attending Evangelist Revival Time Church in Harlem, NY. From an early age, Emanuel had a relationship with God.

Throughout his life, Emanuel experienced many ups and downs. He was incarcerated at one point and made a promise to God that when he was released, he would dedicate his life to Christ and pursue his career as a structural engineer. When Emanuel was released in 1992, he kept his promise.

Emanuel was promoted to Minister in 2022. As a minister, Emanuel desires to live as both a steward and a servant, dedicated to excellence and faithfulness in his calling. His life demonstrates that true success is not only in what we build with our hands but also in what we allow God to build in our hearts.

Emanuel is married to his wife, Dina Owens, and they have four children together.